Practicing the Presence of Jesus

Practicing the Presence of Jesus

Contemporary Meditation

IRENE ALEXANDER

WIPF & STOCK · Eugene, Oregon

PRACTICING THE PRESENCE OF JESUS
Contemporary Meditation

Copyright © 2011 Irene Alexander. All rights reserved. Except for brief quotations in critical publications or reviews, no part of this book may be reproduced in any manner without prior written permission from the publisher. Write: Permissions, Wipf and Stock Publishers, 199 W. 8th Ave., Suite 3, Eugene, OR 97401.

Wipf & Stock
An Imprint of Wipf and Stock Publishers
199 W. 8th Ave., Suite 3
Eugene, OR 97401
www.wipfandstock.com

ISBN 13: 978-1-61097-106-5

Manufactured in the U.S.A.

All scripture quotations, unless otherwise indicated, are taken from the Revised Standard Version of the Bible, copyright 1952 [2nd edition, 1971] by the Division of Christian Education of the National Council of the Churches of Christ in the United States of America. Used by permission. All rights reserved.

*With deep gratitude to my spiritual mothers:
Juanita, Joan, Jean, Lorraine, June,
and, of course, Valerie.*

Contents

Introduction ix

1. Retelling in My Words 1
2. Experiencing the Emotion 12
3. The Emotion Leads to the Story 21
4. Using a Story to Guide My Processing of My Emotion 28
5. Telling Someone Else's Story 32
6. The Older Sister 40
7. Opposites 53
8. A Real Life Experience—and Jesus' Life 65
9. Remembering the Child I Was 75
10. Responding to Art 81
11. Copying the Pattern 87
12. Discerning Both Sides—in Me 93
13. To Be Like Jesus 99
14. Coming to the God Who Is 107
15. Lover and Beloved 113
16. Afterword: A Psychological Understanding of the Transformational Process of Ignatian Composition of Place 122

Bibliography 127

Introduction

ONCE UPON a time, there was a little girl who, as far back as she could remember, knew there was a loving God. She went to church and Sunday school every Sunday and knew that she had to be good. She wanted to be good too, even though she sometimes fought with her brother and sisters, and didn't do what she was told. When she was still quite young, before she could yet read, she had, in the middle of the night one night—who knows why it was at that moment—woken her mother to tell her she wanted to give her heart to Jesus. And then when she could read, and got a Bible of her very own, she read a chapter every day. She found the last verse of Matthew, "Go into all the world . . ." and decided she wanted to be a missionary. She didn't tell anyone—it was her own secret—but it guided her life.

In the Methodist church, where I grew up, being good meant reading the Bible and praying, tithing, and going to church. I read missionary stories, too, and did a class speech about Mary Slessor who went to Africa to "win the hearts of the jungle folk to Christ." I also thought I would go to Africa or India, and that the best thing I could do for God would be to make other people Christians. Even though there were sometimes women lay preachers in the Methodist church, I don't remember ever meeting a woman minister, nor did it occur to me to be trained as one. I was fascinated with people and so went to university to study psychology and counseling, believing those studies would equip me for missionary work.

Instead, psychology gave me a rational scientific worldview and changed my morality into mere conditioning and my spirituality into outdated doctrine—or almost. The charismatic move of the early 1970s swept through New Zealand churches bringing a very present experience of God. I spent my final year of my master's degree completing a practicum in a psychiatric hospital, reading Schaeffer, and trying to bring together my tertiary education, a Christian worldview, and a very real interaction with God.

My childhood dream of becoming a missionary took real shape when I finished my master's degree and joined the international Christian volunteer organization, Youth With A Mission. I met and married a fellow-YWAMer and together we set off for the other side of the world, initially Sweden—not India or Africa but, to our minds, a country just as spiritually dark. The next twelve years were an immersion in community life with different cultures, different countries, and different denominations. Relationships were deep and honest; living without an income developed another way of looking at the world, and the teaching was a whole other education, at the more conservative end of the Christian spectrum but imbued with the reality of lives lived in relationship with God. My husband faced cancer twice and we wrestled with the challenges of faith in the nitty-gritty of ill-health, no money, and living in different countries; but we benefitted from the richness of community relationships, good teaching, and interaction with God.

When we left YWAM to take up "civilian life" again, we struggled to find depth of relationships, authentic church engagement, and a context where our sons could continue to experience a community living out Christian faith. We emigrated to Australia to "start again." While I had been in YWAM, my understanding of missionary had undergone a transformation. My verse "go into all the world and make disciples of all nations," which I had initially understood to mean "convert the heathen," had become an invitation to disciple nations, that is, to influence society in all spheres: business, education, government, health, media, and arts. Tertiary education became an important part of preparing people to influence their society, and a Christian university was therefore essential to help people integrate their faith and their education.

When our sons were teenagers, I embarked on a seven-year journey of doctoral studies investigating epistemic development: how people think about truth and knowledge, how their beliefs in black-and-white truth change over time, and how they find ways to live their truth in a postmodern world. All the while, of course, my own views of truth were changing; I was questioning the fundamentalism I had inherited, and I was seeking ways to know God more authentically. My husband and I came to live in more and more different worlds and when I began to discover the Christian mystics he did not understand.

Like many others who had been through the charismatic renewal of the seventies, or lived the experience of God in the Pentecostal churches, I was not satisfied with an intellectual faith. I sought a deeper knowing of God, and I found many churches to be superficial and glib in their belief systems. Of course, this is a generalization and there are always people who seek God more fully. Many of us are discovering the deeper life of the mystics—men and women through the centuries who had experienced God and called others to richer interaction with the Divine such as Francis of Assisi who showed us how to be instruments of peace in a world of conflict; Theresa of Avila who invited us to mystical union with God while still being very present to the real and needy world around us; John of the Cross, her compatriot, who taught us that the "dark night of the soul" leads us to God "more surely than the dawn"; Ignatius of Loyola who showed us how to put ourselves into the gospel stories with all our senses. This is the "composition of place," which I am attempting to demonstrate through the following pages.

Many of us are also discovering spiritual direction: the relationship in which one person opens a hospitable and accepting place for the other to explore more deeply their relationship with God. Spiritual direction, or companioning, has been part of Christian life for millennia, right back to when the city people sought out the desert fathers and mothers to help them find the presence of the Spirit in their lives. I have found it to be deeply respectful of the work of the Spirit in my life, but in a different way from that of the discipling I had practiced in YWAM or of the Christian counseling I taught in our courses. Spiritual direction, as I have experienced it, emphasizes the contemplative—the listening to the still small voice in my inner being, the presence of the Spirit who calls me to attentiveness to the movements of life within my spirit. As evangelicals and Pentecostals, we have often been more impressed with the external Word and the tongues of fire of the Spirit's tangible presence than with silence and a contemplative space. The spiritual directors who have journeyed with me have been women of prayer and sensitivity, women who know, in Rizzuto's phrase, the importance of "exquisite attention to the experience"[1] of the person.

In the following pages, I have given examples of my own interactions with the scriptures using my version of Ignatius of Loyola's method. I put myself into the story, imagining what it was like to actually be there—picturing the sounds, sights, smells (the reality of everyday life), and most of all, finding within myself the emotional reactions, the hurts, fears, anger, and pain of the people who interacted with Jesus—and thus bringing the reality of my own lived experience into the presence of the One who opens a compassionate space to give exquisite attention, to tenderly heal, and to deeply challenge.

Emotions are the motivators of our lives, and the deepest satisfaction. God is a God of deep grief, of joy that bursts into song, of anger, of extravagant romantic love. Life without emotions is colorless and boring. It is emotion that gives us life. We are meant to be fully rounded beings, as God is, with emotion, reason, imagination, choices. It is the balance that is the goal. Those with deep spiritual lives know what it is to engage with their emotions in God's presence. "Oh," says Jeremiah, "that my eyes were a fountain

---

1. Rizzuto, *Birth of the Living God*, 211.

of tears."[2] "I will joy over them with singing," Zephaniah[3] quotes God as saying. "I am sorry that I made them," says God with a sigh that is like a gasp for air.[4] "I am sick with love," say the lovers in Solomon's song.[5] When the people hear the prophets, they beat their breasts and repent with sack cloth and ashes.[6] We too are designed to experience stories—and God—with our emotions.

Jesus constantly uses story; He is constantly imagining ways to get across to the people truths that are difficult, if not impossible to express in rational, technical language. The kingdom of heaven is like . . . And now use your imagination. It is story, and poetry, movies, and music that call to our deepest being, call us to change and commitment, call us to surrender and to act nobly. Somehow we, children of the West, have thought our God was a rational God who only met us through correct theology. (For a further explanation of the psychological transformational process of the Ignatian method, see the final chapter.)

The chapters that follow are true to the scriptures as we have them, but my imagination fills out the stories. I am certainly not claiming that what I imagine is what happened. I am seeking to find God through the stories we have. I hope that my stories and experiences will spark for others a deeper engagement with the God of these stories, the God who grieves with our losses, and laughs in delight with our joy.

2. Jer 9:1.
3. Zeph 3:17.
4. Gen 6:6.
5. Song 5:8.
6. Jer 39:19.

1

Retelling in My Words

FINDING WAYS TO BE INSIDE THE GOSPEL

Many of us have read and reread the gospel stories; maybe we heard them in our youth, and know them from as far back as we remember. If so, it is likely we have identified at some level with the characters in the story, imagined ourselves sitting at the feet of Jesus with Mary of Bethany, identified with the disciples in the storm, questioned if we would have run away in the Garden of Gethsemane. Sometimes we have found fresh insight as we listen again, other times we may wonder if we have mined all we can from the stories. We may need to find new ways to slip through the curtain separating us from the real human world that Jesus walked in. One way to slip through the curtain is to retell the story in our own words, to imagine writing in a journal as one of the characters, or pen a letter to a friend. We might specifically select a story that parallels our own life in some way, or simply choose a story that seems to invite our attention.

Recognizing My Own Need for Resurrection

My academic work has been a source of life to me. To see other people gain understanding, experience the self-knowledge of their own transformational journey, developing courses to facilitate this process, and coordinate the work of others to contribute to the overall program is very satisfying—but also life-consuming. After fourteen years of academic work, which had included the end of my marriage, I knew I needed a sabbatical. Exactly what I would do was unclear, except for one thing; I knew I wanted to take part in a thirty-day silent retreat. I had already experienced a number of shorter retreats and found them deeply challenging and deeply life-giving. I eventually found a retreat center set amongst mountainous beauty, and the spiritual companionship of a gentle and steadfast nun.

As the days passed and I faced some of my demons, I came to have recognition of my own despair. My director suggested I spend the day contemplating the subjects of death and resurrection. I set off for a three hour walk around the lake taking with me the story of Martha and Lazarus. I was only too aware of the losses in my own life and the death of my dreams; so it was easy to imagine myself as Martha experiencing the loss of her dearly beloved brother. It was also easy to imagine the disciples' fears of losing Jesus. As I put myself in Martha's shoes, I imagined her retelling her story to a friend, or pouring out her feelings into a diary.

As I pondered on the image of Martha asking Jesus to come to save her brother from dying, I could feel how heartrending her brother's loss would have been for her, how empty her life would be without him, how she could not bear to imagine it. As I connected with this image, I allowed my own fears of losing what was most precious to me to come to the surface. This enabled me to bring those fears to Jesus in a very real way.

I also imagined what it would have been like to be present as Jesus and the disciples received Martha's messenger, and put myself into the person of Mary Magdalene, listening and responding in fear of loss of the man she loved.

DARING TO BELIEVE RESURRECTION (JOHN 11)

Martha:

My brother is dying. Every day he is weaker and there is nothing that helps. Even physicians who know about this sickness say there is nothing we can do. We are taking turns to sit with him. But I cannot sleep. I cannot bear for him to die. He and Mary and I have stayed together since our parents died. We've had enough money to do it. We have felt so right together. Even though others have pressured me, I have not married; I want to stay with my brother and sister. And now he is dying. How will we live without him?

There is one thing I can do. It will endanger a dear friend, but I must do it. I cannot bear that he should die. I'll send a servant; Joshua would be best. First thing in the morning he can go and find Jesus. I know it's dangerous for Jesus to come here, so close to Jerusalem. And he may not come. But I can no longer bear not to ask. And I know he loves Lazarus as I do. I can only ask.

Mary Magdalene:

Who is this late at night, asking for Jesus? I think I recognize him; ah, I know him. He's a servant of Lazarus and Martha. He's being shown to the room where they're talking, discussing the day and tomorrow's plans. I can hear him telling of Lazarus's sickness—and Martha's request that Jesus come. No! I hold my breath willing him to say no. It's much too dangerous, and I hear Thomas saying so: "What! When we know the Pharisees in Jerusalem are out to get him!"

Jesus is quiet. I can imagine him looking at each one in turn—his penetrating look that makes each of us search our reactions and our motives.

He does not answer. Then he says to the servant, "Stay with us tonight, and tell Martha we received the message." He said this with great kindness, but with no hint of a response. Please Jesus, you mustn't go.

The next morning I am tense, afraid he will be setting off with the servant, but I see the man leave alone. Jesus obviously has other plans. Over the next two days I relax as he seems to be making no preparations to leave.

Martha:

What shall I do? I've done everything. I'm exhausted but I cannot sleep. My tears are cried out. I keep as busy as I can. And I cannot help saying it: I wish Jesus had come. I know it's dangerous. I know he has to make these decisions. But I know he could have prevented him from dying. Lazarus is dead. I cannot bear it. Why didn't he come? Joshua told me he just said, "Tell her I got the message. Tell her to trust." So what did that mean? I did all the trusting I could, but Lazarus is dead. And yet even now, even now, if only he would come. I heard he brought back the widow's son. I'm going to have to send Joshua again. I can't bear to not tell Jesus. I'll just tell him to say Lazarus is dead. Then it's up to him. And, meantime, I've sent messages to everyone in the village and Jerusalem. I've cooked, and organized, and planned. Tomorrow we will bury him. I cannot bear it. Oh Jesus, please come, at least to comfort us.

Mary Magdalene:

Here's Martha's servant again. I see the others tense up as well. None of us want Jesus to go up there. I can't hear the servant's message but then I hear Jesus say, "Our friend Lazarus is sleeping." I hear Peter's relieved laugh, "Great he's on the mend then." We all relax, but only for a moment. "No, I mean he has died. And for your sakes, I'm glad I wasn't there, because now you will believe. So let us go to him."

What! What is he talking about? Lazarus is dead. My heart weeps for Martha and Mary. But they would understand. Jesus cannot go there now. Then Thomas says it for all of us. "Let's also go, that we might die with him." He knows there's no point in trying to persuade Jesus, and so we begin to prepare to leave. I'm going to go up there, too; I can't let this happen and not be there.

Martha:

> We have buried him. My life is empty, even though everyone's still here, even though we've eaten and drunk and told stories of him, and sung together. How will life go on?
>
> And Mary. Mary of course is beside herself. She can't stop crying. I didn't even tell her I sent Joshua again. I didn't want her to hope. I know that's all she thinks about—"If only Jesus had been here. If only he was here now."
>
> I'm giving up hope of him coming. Lazarus has been dead for four days; he would surely have come by now if he was coming. Except Joshua isn't back yet, and I have the tiniest hope that it's because Jesus is coming, and that they're all coming together. I keep looking out the window, just in case, and even though I tell myself not to hope. I guess I'm afraid that if I really let go of that hope, there really will be nothing to live for.
>
> Wait. I can see Joshua coming. He's alone. But still, maybe . . . I'm going to go out and meet him.

Letting Hope Lead

So Martha goes and finds, to her joy, that Jesus and the disciples are not far off: one last rest stop before facing whatever will meet them at Bethany. She can hardly stop herself from running to where Joshua points for her to go.

FINDING RESURRECTION

Martha:

I can't wait any longer. I can't even go back and tell Mary. I just have to give Joshua a whole list of instructions for the kitchen for extra food, and then run. When I finally see him—oh, I am rude. I don't even thank him for coming, I just burst into tears and blurt, "Lord, if you had been here my brother would not have died." I look up through my tears, into those eyes of his, and from my heart comes my longing, "And even now I know that whatever you ask from God, God will give you."

He replies, "Martha, your brother will rise again." Steady, intent.

I slow down. It is as though the world has stopped. His eyes could make you believe anything. And yet I don't dare. I stumble out the only answer I can give with any sort of certainty, "I know he will rise again in the resurrection at the last day."

He looks at me again, long and slow. It is as though my heart slows and nothing else exists.

"I am the resurrection and the life; he who believes in me, though he die, yet shall he live, and whoever lives and believes in me shall never die."

What claim is this he is making?

And then he challenges me, "Do you believe this?"

How could I not? With him there holding the world still. With all my heart I believe everything.

"Yes Lord, I believe that you are the Christ, the Son of God, he who is coming into the world."

When I say this, it is as though the world begins to move again, but still with something changed forever. Something within me stills to a steady bedrock. He understands, that smile that just holds you. Then he asks about Mary and I remember that other people exist.

"I'll go and get her," I tell him.

As I hurry back, I want to laugh and cry at the same time. I don't know what it means. I hardly even knew *how* to think of what Jesus had meant about Lazarus. I just know that what I'd said was true. He is the Christ. Oh, I know we have been saying that for a while—those of us who really know him. But did we know what we were saying? He, the Christ, who all the Ages have been waiting for. The joy within me bursts, but I don't know how to say any of it. All I can do when I get back is to call Mary aside and tell her Jesus is here. I hardly even tell her where he is before she is gone, running, hair flying. The people begin to follow. I don't stop them. What could I say?

I go to the kitchen to make sure everything is being prepared before I too set off back. I don't want to miss a moment of what Jesus is saying. By the time I catch up, Mary is already there. She is as bad as I had been, no, worse. She falls sobbing at Jesus' feet and says, "Lord, if you had been here my brother would not have died."

The others who gather around her are in tears, too. And Jesus looks at Mary, and looks at her deep grief and he, too, is in tears. No conversation about resurrection with her. Just his arms around her, and tears running down his face. "Where have you laid him?" he asks.

Someone says they'll show the way and I can hear others talking as we all follow. "See how he loved him," says someone, moved by Jesus' tears. And others, voicing what Mary and I had said: "Couldn't he have stopped him from dying?" "Why didn't he come before?"

It doesn't take us long to get to the tomb. We all stop at the entrance. Mary sobs on Jesus' arm and Jesus holds her and weeps, too. Then he says, "Take away the stone."

I step forward—surely he doesn't need to go in. "Lord, he's been dead four days. Really, it will smell very badly," I say.

Jesus looks at me, that long look. "Didn't I tell you that if you believe you would see the glory of God?"

Could this really be what he meant? Somehow I didn't dare even think it. Yet, those eyes; I had to respond. I turn and tell some of the men to help with the stone.

And Jesus just stands there. Then he looks up to heaven, as we'd seen him do so many times. He talks to God in that intimate way of his, "Father I thank you that you have heard me." We are all silent. Even Mary stops crying and stares at him. It is as though we are straining our mortal minds to understand something only the angels comprehend.

And then he cries out, "Lazarus, come out!"

We all stand frozen. I don't know what we expect. I don't know what I expect. We all just stand, staring.

And then suddenly, there is Lazarus. All bound in the bandages I myself had wrapped—but standing. Only Jesus can speak, "Unbind him and let him go."

Somehow people move again and they begin to unwrap him.

I drag my eyes away and look at Jesus' face. He is looking at me, a smile, and yet a joy. It is the look I've seen before when someone has finally understood something he was trying to explain, almost— the "Didn't I tell you?" look—and yet with such kindness that your heart jumps to respond. He looks at me like that, as if he is saying, "This is what you expected, wasn't it, Martha; this is what you knew." And all of my being is dumb with astonishment; how could I claim to have even begun to understand.

By now, they have taken the bandages off Lazarus and when I look back at his face I see he and Jesus exchange a look I cannot describe, one of the deepest understanding and of a joy unimaginable, as though they share a secret no one else could ever understand.

And Lazarus's face, it was more alive than I have ever seen it. I, who closed those eyes in death just four days ago, the life in them now is as though he will never die. The thought comes to my mind, "He knows what Jesus means when he says he's the resurrection." These two, they know something the rest of us are just beginning to get an inkling of. Except Mary; maybe Mary, too. The look on her face is like sunlight. Everyone around me is talking at once. But those three—their faces are teaching my heart to believe the words I uttered, "You are the Christ, the Son of God."

LETTING MARTHA'S EXPERIENCE TRANSFORM MINE

As I walked with each of the people in the story, feeling my own despair and fear and speaking the truth about them, I began to experience something of the transformation. This was not something I could do quickly, nor was it something I could do simply by thinking about it objectively. Feeling the emotions and bringing them gently into God's presence took time. Being with his responses, seeing where they led, experiencing the flow of understanding and gentle healing was a slow and ongoing process, but one made real by the story and the questioning of what it would have been like to live it.

2

Experiencing the Emotion

IDENTIFICATION LEADS TO TRANSFORMATION

ONE OF the most powerful effects when identifying with gospel stories is that we can find ourselves transformed—emotionally healed by the interaction with this incarnate God whom we experience in the story. Many of us have learned to read the gospel stories with our reason, analyzing the events and the meaning. A much deeper way to read them is to add the emotional dimension. To imagine what this person must have been feeling and to find the part of myself that identifies with that emotion. As we do this, we bring those places where pain and wounds live within us into the presence of the Jesus of the story, the same Jesus who responds in the present. Although we may have read the story many times, the experience of identification means we encounter it in a new way.

Engaging with Pain and Shame

My marriage breakup, and the events surrounding it, took me on a deep journey to places of pain, rejection, and shame, leading to self-reflection. I sought God more intensely than I ever had. Most hurtful were the judgments of other Christians who believed that I was "in deception" or "in sin." Deeply disturbing were my own fears that they might possibly be right. Julian of Norwich's words, "Give me of yourself else I shall ever be in want," became my prayer, especially as I found myself wanting to turn to other men for comfort. My mantra became "God, it is you that I want."

As I continued to learn to put myself into gospel stories, I experienced the reality of Jesus responding to my longing, my fear, and my shame. By enfleshing these feelings in the very human stories of the gospels, I found the incarnate God touching me deeply in the reality of my daily life. My own deep emotions enabled me to recognize the depth of the emotions of the real people of these biblical stories, and to be present with them in their encounters with the Jesus of history and eternity.

The biblical story of the bent-over woman, which had previously been a story of healing and Sabbath-keeping, became for me a story of shame and sacrifice. Because I so quickly blame myself for things that are wrong, I could easily imagine that she blamed herself for her physical condition, and read judgment and rejection in the responses of those around her. I identify with the shame I imagine her carrying, and I follow her story through to her encounter with a man who sees her real inner being.

THE SHAME THAT BURDENS

And there was a woman who had had a spirit of infirmity for eighteen years; she was bent over and could not fully straighten herself. And when Jesus saw her, he called her and said to her, "Woman, you are freed from your infirmity." And he laid his hands upon her, and immediately she was made straight, and she praised God. But the ruler of the synagogue, indignant because Jesus had healed on the Sabbath, said to the people, "There are six days on which work ought to be done; come on those days and be healed, and not on the Sabbath day." Then the Lord answered him, "You hypocrites! Does not each of you on the Sabbath untie his ox or his ass from the manger, and lead it away to water it? And ought not this woman, a daughter of Abraham whom Satan bound for eighteen years, be loosed from this bond on the Sabbath day?" As he said this, all his adversaries were put to shame (Luke 13:11–17).

Shame
for eighteen years
bent double.
Oh the shame.
What a sinner she,
That God should visit on her such punishment.
She knew they thought that.
Even if they did not say it outright—
Whispered it behind their hands,
Thought it behind their self-righteous looks,
That somehow she was to blame.
She had gone to God

over and over.
What have I done?
What can I repent of?
What secret sin have I committed?
What secret look given?
What secret thought thought?
God show me that I may repent.
And sometimes there was peace—I have done all I know.
And sometimes there was turmoil—
Is there yet some hidden thing,
Something unrepented,
Some pride held?

Eighteen years.
Her shame evident—
Carried in a secret place.

She expected to go to her grave bent double,
Expected only to be remembered as the bent one.
The spark of love in her eyes known only by a few.
Shunned by most.
Who would befriend such a one?
But she still faithfully went to the synagogue.
Faithfully she found her silent way amongst the clamor of life.
Faithfully cared for herself and sometimes gave what little help she could, minding a sleeping child here,
or sitting with a sick one there
—at least she could call for help if it was needed.
But mostly alone. Mostly silent.
Mostly waiting out the years.

Then she heard of a healer.

She'd heard of others, and hovered at the back of the crowd.
Ignored,
Pushed past,
Overlooked,
Unseen,
Invisible.
. . . She'd go and listen again.

He saw her.
Somehow he saw her.
How did he do that?
Was he looking for ones such as she?
He who came poor from heaven, did he look for those bent double?
He saw her, and called her to him,
"Come daughter of Sarah,
Come faithful one.
I am Son of my Father.
I see your heart toward me,
I see your faith.
I see your doubts.
I see you,
I see you, daughter."

He called her.
He laid his hands on her.
Not for the crowd,
Not for the praise,
Not for the show.
He sees the little ones.
The bent and broken.
That's what he came for.
And she?

She went home dancing.
While he
was left to argue
with the religious ones.
"Do you not untie your donkey on the Sabbath?
The Sabbath that was made for man, not man for
the Sabbath.
The Sabbath that was made for freedom.
And she a daughter of Sarah, may I not untie her
on the Sabbath?"

Eventually they got him for it.
Eventually they killed him.
"Ha, you Sabbath breaker,
You who breaks the rules,
Now you are broken."

He came poor.
He became broken.
But he set me free.

From General to Specific, Becoming Naked

The way I wrote this poem was more general. Imagining what it would be like to be a bent over one, a shamed one, one who did not measure up, in some impossible way.

But I have found it is very helpful to be more specific—to name the reality of shame in my own life. The shame may be from my own self-judgements, some brokenness or hurt, or rejection of my own. Or it may be from without: from society's standards, from my religion's beliefs, from our patriarchal culture, or from my own family's particular expectations. And some of society's standards will be internalized, and will be an ever present critic that adds to the burdens and to my bentness.

So, I later rewrote the story of the bent-over woman, this time naming the specifics of the shame involved in my marriage break-up—the shame that I could not make it work. The scriptures only seemed to name adultery as reason for divorce, and that did not apply in our case. However much I studied the Greek words and tried to justify myself, I was still left wanting; I could no longer see myself as upright.

I have found that the key is to go towards the pain, to sense where the tears are and to stay with them. Name them. And bring them into the presence of the compassionate God. Stay with the story. Stay with the reality of Jesus' response.

REVISITING THE SHAME THAT BURDENS

Shame
A Christian
A leader
An educated woman
A counselor
If you can't work out your marriage who can?

Shame
How can you expect to help others if you can't even help yourself?
How can you expect to have any authority, if you don't work it out in your own life?

Shame
Don't you know God hates divorce?
Don't you know that divorce is only because you are hard of heart?
Don't you know the Bible says . . .

And I am bent with carrying this, these twelve, fifteen, eighteen years.

Shame.
Jesus I come to you.
Bent with my own brokenness,
and bent with the shame others have heaped upon me.
And I come on this Sabbath day.
This holy day
When, of all days, men must say what the scriptures say,
do what the scriptures demand.
And scriptures demand that you not lift a finger to carry my burden.
After all it is a Sabbath and one must not take burdens on the Sabbath.
And the scriptures say—do they not?—that only if there has been adultery . . .
God I am broken and burdened
And I can no longer stand upright.
I am no longer upright
I come to you knowing only how to endure, how to persevere.

Jesus breaks the law.
He looks into my eyes—and breaks the law.
He lifts my burden.

He takes away my condemnation
and I can stand straight
and look God in the eye.
Oh, not because suddenly I have become righteous.
Not because I can tell you the real Greek meanings of the words.
Not because I know the law better than the righteous ones.
Just because my brokenness does not faze him.
Because my self-condemnation is not from him.
Because it is for him, not me, to argue with the religious ones.
And I, I shall keep my eyes on his.
Keep my ears attuned to his music,
And I shall dance
Dance into the kingdom of heaven
Which is made for the little ones,
the broken ones,

the ones who cannot help themselves.

RECEIVING THE HEALING

The more honest I am, the more specifically I name my woundedness, the more I am able to receive the healing of the One who calls me to him—he who looks me in the eye and gives me freedom. Writing in free poetry can allow the words, and so the emotions, to come more freely. So, I find myself seen for who I am, my bentness named and surrendered, my accusing voices answered by the Crucified One.

3

The Emotion Leads to the Story

LETTING THE EMOTION LEAD THE WAY

IN THE last chapter, I took a story and imagined how it would feel to be that person, allowing that process to touch my own similar feelings. In this chapter, I demonstrate the process of starting with my own emotion and letting the emotion lead me to a relevant story. This becomes an intentional way of inviting the Holy Spirit to touch and heal a specific place of struggle or questioning.

When I have used this process with others, I have been struck with how precisely their emotion leads to the relevant story. We are so used to analyzing and choosing rationally, so taking a little time to be with the emotion first is helpful. We can name the emotion, notice where it is present in our body, or describe its color or shape. This focus enables our heart, God's spirit within, to lead us to a story that fits the challenge we are experiencing.

My "Good Enough" Question Leads to the Bleeding Woman

I first discovered the Ignatian process (truly identifying with the people in a gospel story) when I started spiritual direction. As a good evangelical protestant, I had read my Bible daily, had chosen to believe the truth of the Word, and had made right choices in response to the morals portrayed in it. A friend had explained to me what spiritual direction is; it is not really a direction but more a companioning, with a focus on my relationship with God. Spiritual direction is not counseling (with its problem focus) and it is not discipling, either (with its tendency to direct in the "right" way). To try to achieve a better understanding of what it could mean for me, I made an appointment with Juanita, a very down-to-earth nun who offended me the first time I saw her by talking about "your God"—as if "my" God was different from other people's, or different from her Catholic one. On reflection, though, I realized that she spoke of "your God" as a very respectful acknowledgement that she was not trying to make me believe in "her God," or anyone else's, but was deeply honoring my journey and my spirituality.

As I came to trust Juanita, I told her of my struggle with several things: questioning whether I was good enough, questioning whether God really accepted me, and fearing that there might be some hidden cause that I didn't know about that would cause God to judge me. I experienced this feeling of judgment, even though I had had a "personal relationship with God" for forty-five years, had earned a doctorate degree, and currently held a respected job in a Christian organization.

"This sounds like a little fox," said Juanita, alluding to the "little foxes that spoil the vines" in Song of Solomon.[1] "This isn't a little fox," I told her, "this is a big fox; this is a wolf I've struggled with all my life."

1. Song 2:15.

"Ah," she said, "I wonder if we could try finding a story for it. Would you like to try that?" As I agreed, she explained that I should focus on the emotion. Really notice what it was like, where it was I carried it in my body, how it made me feel about myself. Then she told me to let it lead me to a gospel story. Who in the gospels felt like this? This was not to be an analytical process, I was simply to let the feeling lead me to someone from the Bible who also felt inadequate and unconvinced she "had what it takes," someone who questioned whether she would be accepted or acceptable.

The story that came to me was about the woman with twelve years of bleeding. She was afraid to come out openly, she was afraid of what people would think. She didn't know if she would be acceptable. She carried a hidden shame, a hidden woundedness, a fear of rejection, a fear that she deserved rejection. I didn't yet analyze all of this; I simply let my awareness of my feeling connect me with this woman who looked for healing for her hidden brokenness.

I knew the story well enough to immediately know Jesus' response.

> And a woman who had had a flow of blood for twelve years and could not be healed by any one, came up behind him, and touched the fringe of his garment; and immediately her flow of blood ceased. And Jesus said, "Who was it that touched me?" When all denied it, Peter said, "Master, the multitudes surround you and press upon you!" But Jesus said, "Someone touched me; for I perceive that power has gone forth from me." And when the woman saw that she was not hidden, she came trembling, and falling down before him

> declared in the presence of all the people why she had touched him, and how she had been immediately healed. And he said to her, "Daughter, your faith has made you well; go in peace" (Luke 8:43–48).

As I envisioned myself in this story, my sense of Jesus' response to me, and mine to him, was almost instantaneous. As soon as I allowed myself inside this story, identifying with the bleeding woman and imagining myself there, I experienced Jesus' response: his acceptance of me and his honoring of me.

THE EXCLUDED ONE IS WELCOMED

> All I bring, Father, is my feeling—my awareness of how I feel—my sensing of my own need. And I bring it with cupped hands to you.
>   Here is my sense of inadequacy, my fear that I haven't got what it takes, that you may not be interested in me. I bring it to you.

And I think of someone in the gospels who felt like that.

I think of the woman with twelve years of bleeding: her fear of losing life, her desperation to find healing—her situation only getting worse. She didn't know if she was good enough. She didn't plan to come face to face with Jesus.

And she came in trepidation, in secrecy, anonymous in the crowd, shrouding herself from recognition, and with the longing of faith she touched Jesus' garment—only the hem of his garment. That touch was enough to heal twelve years of sickness.

Abundant life.
In just the hem of his garment.
The edges of his ways.

Looking at the Process

Afterwards, I tried to slow the process down, to visit the story again, and explain what had happened.

RETELLING TO SEE THE PROCESS

I bring *my* feeling to him, cupped in my hands and I see Jesus' response.

Jesus is the father. Jesus is God made flesh so we can see. So the distortions are transformed. And we see him in truth.

> Jesus turns and seeks me out. Who is it that touched me? Touched me with the faith of one in need. Seeking life.
>
> And finding myself recognized, knowing I have found healing, found life, I dare to take aside my shroud, dare the stares of the crowd, and say, "It was I, Lord. I come to you. In you is life. In you alone. Nowhere else. You alone have the words of eternal life; where else would I go?"
>
> I meet his eyes. My faith, my daring to believe reflected in my look.
>
> And his, the eyes of a lover. Alone in the crowd.
>
> His eyes give life. His eyes recognize me, the essential me.
>
> He looks into my heart. And I am good enough, good enough because I am made by him and my longing, my deep heart's longing, is for him.

And he lifts me up and says, "Your faith has made
  you whole."
And my heart sings.
I have found him.
Him whom my soul has longed for.
The life-giver.

JESUS SEEKS FULL HEALING

Over the years, this story has continued to resonate with me. Having experienced it from "the inside," I gained understanding of what Jesus was doing in seeking out the "one who touched him." Although Peter said, "Everyone is touching you, Lord," Jesus still insisted on finding who it was. I have questioned what that would be like for this woman. She would have been considered unclean, because she was bleeding. Unclean for twelve years, what a burden to bear. What a wearying, shaming label. So, in pushing through the crowd, she was making others unclean. And Jesus wanted her to identify herself—publicly. I am convinced it was because he wanted to complete the healing. This was not just a physical healing, it was psychological as well. And he was not going to let her leave only partially healed. He insisted on knowing who the person was. He heard her story and then publicly honored her in front of the whole crowd, even though he and his disciples were in a hurry to get to Jairus's house. But he stopped so that he could honor her. "Your faith has made you whole. Your faith. What you did. Your boldness. Your breaking the rules. Your overcoming your own shame, and fear, and condemnation. You are made whole. I honor you."

As I emotionally identify with this woman and hold out my need to Jesus, I too am honored. The part of me that is courageous, and bold, and willing to go against the other parts of me that condemn and silence is honored. And I take hold of Jesus' honoring. And when the old doubts come up, I remind myself. I am good enough. My Creator and my Beloved have declared it, in front of everyone. All I need to do is touch the edges of his presence to remind myself. I am made whole; I do not need to allow my life to hemorrhage away. I choose to stand before the crowds of my self-condemning thoughts and be whole.

There are similarities between this process and that one used in healing prayer, in prayer where "Jesus is invited into the story of the person's pain." This is a very effective healing process. The difference with this process is that the gospel story is the story. Neither the pray-er nor the one being prayed for "makes up" a picture or story of Jesus' response. The gospel story simply states it. In this way, this process is a very "safe" one. I cannot be imagining a God other than the one the gospel tells of because the gospel itself tells Jesus' response. Then, if there is ever a question of whether "I have just made this up," I can go back to the Bible. Here is what Jesus is like. Here is how Jesus responds to those such as me, who need healing, who long for his touch, who are inadequate in themselves.

4

Using a Story to Guide My Processing of My Emotion

FOLLOWING THE LEAD OF ANOTHER'S EXPERIENCES

SOMETIMES LIFE seems to be taking us nowhere. We know we are stuck, we want to move forward, but the same patterns keep recurring, the same thoughts come over and over, the tape replays repeatedly. At times like this we need something from the outside to lead us forward: someone else's story to follow, a different starting place to come to God.

Letting the Story Lead Me

As I learned the process of letting my emotions take me to a gospel story, I began to use it when I was faced with difficulty, pain, or something unresolved. One day in particular I had expected to meet with someone who I thought would be helpful to me, but they did not come. I was left waiting, and thinking, alone. As I waited, I noticed the patterns of my thinking, of my pain and self-blame, going round and round. I could find no way forward and felt paralyzed in my own inability to move. I let this feeling take me to a story (included at the end of this chapter). I simply let the gospel story lead me through the naming of my paralysis, and I wrote down my reality of that moment and my responses. This time I hardly talked about the gospel setting at all. If you did not know that I was following the story, it might simply read like a journal entry—which it was.

WAITING, PARALYZED

I sit and wait.
Another day, another waiting.
Each day. Waiting
Waiting for change that doesn't come.
Stuck in the same old patterns—around and around in my head.
Paralyzed by my pain, my regret, my grief, my wanting something I cannot have, my disappointment.
I fill my days with busy-ness, other people's needs, I listen to their talk, but my own I cannot heal.
I half listen. I give what I can. But I know I am stuck—in a half-giving, because I cannot let go, I do not know how to go forward. I wish I could live my life again. I would make different decisions. I would not take the way that led thus . . . but what I have done, I have done.
My friends come, saying they've found an answer. You should read this book, do this course, come to this church, meet this man. I do not share their excitement, their faith.
But I'll let them carry me along with them. And I am grateful for friends, grateful for their hope, grateful for their caring for me.

There is a crowd, and I don't like crowds. I feel exposed, vulnerable. I have to put on my mask—my exterior face. So they do not see the brokenness within, the stuckness, the paralysis, the disappointment.

But my friends push on oblivious—it is not their paralysis on show.

They put me down in the middle of it all. And I am alone. Unmasked and exposed.

I look into the face of a man who is different. He is silent, looking deeply into my eyes. And he sees everything. There is no hiding from those eyes.

And I find I do not want to hide. Let him see the brokenness, the paralysis, the half-finished dreams, the impossibilities. I let him see. It is all laid bare. This is who I am. You know it, I know it. Here is all there is.

For I somehow know these eyes do not look in judgment—and even if they did—well I can do no other. God, this is not what I meant to do with my life. But here I am. This is what I have done. This is who I am. I throw myself on your mercy. There is no other way. If there had been, I would have done it! But no.

He looks deeply. Take heart; be encouraged; have hope. Listen to your heart—the inklings of hope there. Take heart; it's okay; all be well; all will be very well.

Take heart, your sins are forgiven. All the things that come between you and God, between you and life, between you and freedom—they are removed. There is nothing that can separate you.

All you have done—I see your heart. I see your longing, I too know that longing.

> And so you may know all this is true: Rise, take up your bed and go home. Act on it. Rise up. Take heart. Walk it out.

THE STORY GIVES A WAY FORWARD

> And behold, they brought to him a paralytic, lying on his bed; and when Jesus saw their faith he said to the paralytic, "Take heart, my son; your sins are forgiven." And behold, some of the scribes said to themselves, "This man is blaspheming." But Jesus, knowing their thoughts, said, "Why do you think evil in your hearts? For which is easier, to say, 'Your sins are forgiven,' or to say, 'Rise and walk'? But that you may know that the Son of man has authority on earth to forgive sins"—he then said to the paralytic—"Rise, take up your bed and go home." And he rose and went home (Matt 9:2–7).

This time I have used the story as a frame and put my content into it. It was my recognition of how I go over and over things in my head. And indeed it was a day of waiting. And as I waited, I noticed the rehashing, the stuckness—and so I let it take me to the paralyzed man. How was I like him? . . . And then having had identified with him, I identified my feelings and brought those into the presence of Jesus. And what does Jesus say? Take heart. What might that mean for me? Your sins are forgiven? What might that mean: all that stands between me and life, freedom, God, wholeness. What would it be like for me to take hold of that, to put aside those things? Here is a challenge to take away with me.

5

Telling Someone Else's Story

COMING INDIRECTLY

Letting our problem or pain lead us to a story can be a powerful way to process what we need to face. I have found, though, that sometimes the story or the person I come to may present some difficulty for me. For some reason, I have difficulty identifying with that person directly. That person may seem too different, too far ahead of me in the journey, too able to do the very thing I am struggling with doing. I have found that an easier way to identify with that person is to come at it "sideways." One way to do this is to imagine myself as someone present in the story but not the main character—someone to identify with who is observing or present but less central in the story.

Watching Another Instead of Myself

An example of this "sideways" processing is when I identified with the story of Mary when she became pregnant with Jesus, as told by her kinswoman Elizabeth. I wrote this one day when I had realized that a recurring theme for me was that of not being deserving. However much I would tell myself that it is not about being deserving, I would discover it just under the surface yet again. As I pondered which story to go to, I thought of Mary—conscious that she was a mere village girl, yet visited by Almighty God not because she was deserving, but because the Almighty is a God of grace.

The difficulty was that the very problem I was struggling with—deserving to be visited by Almighty God—somehow seemed so straightforward for her; whereas, it was anything but straightforward for me. As I read the passage again I began to wonder how it might have been for Elizabeth, herself pregnant, hearing Mary's song. So, I decided to try Mary's story told from Elizabeth's perspective. This is the story of "Mary's Song: The Magnificat," the theme of which is God wanting to bring the Word to flesh in all of humanity. The idea is that each person, in responding to God, can be "pregnant with the holy."

> After these days his wife Elizabeth conceived, and for five months she hid herself, saying, "Thus the Lord has done to me in the days when he looked on me, to take away my reproach among men."
>
> . . . In those days Mary arose and went with haste into the hill country, to a city of Judah, and she entered the house of Zechariah and greeted Elizabeth. And when Elizabeth heard the greeting of Mary, the babe leaped in her womb; and Elizabeth was filled with the Holy Spirit and she exclaimed with a loud cry, "Blessed are you among women, and blessed is the fruit of your womb! And why is this granted me, that the mother of my Lord should come to me? For behold, when the voice of your greeting came to my ears, the babe in my womb leaped for joy. And blessed is

she who believed that there would be a fulfillment of what was spoken to her from the Lord." And Mary said, "My soul magnifies the Lord, and my spirit rejoices in God my Savior, for he has regarded the low estate of his handmaiden. For behold, henceforth all generations will call me blessed; for he who is mighty has done great things for me, and holy is his name. And his mercy is on those who fear him from generation to generation. He has shown strength with his arm, he has scattered the proud in the imagination of their hearts, he has put down the mighty from their thrones, and exalted those of low degree; he has filled the hungry with good things, and the rich he has sent empty away. He has helped his servant Israel, in remembrance of his mercy, as he spoke to our fathers, to Abraham and to his posterity for ever." And Mary remained with her about three months, and returned to her home (Luke 1:24–25, 39–56).

ELIZABETH'S STORY

When I found I was pregnant for sure, something seemed to settle down deeply inside me. Right at the beginning, when Zechariah came home from his turn at the temple and couldn't speak I knew something profound had happened. He's always been a spiritual man, but not given to religious experiences, and nothing like this had ever happened to him before. It was enough to convince me, even though I had come to terms with my barrenness years ago.

Oh, at first it wasn't like that. Like any young wife I wanted to be pregnant; I wanted to give my husband children and my parents grandchildren. So each month I would hope, and then be disappointed. Month after month: disappointment and shame. Obviously, everyone knows. And I questioned God: was there something I was doing wrong; was this some curse? And I begged him, and complained. And I told him it wasn't fair. I said things to him other people might have been shocked at. But I learned how to go into God's presence and find his peace. It took me years, though.

It's a reproach being barren. You know that people believe you're not fulfilling God's purpose. Not only that, it's an ache in your heart that doesn't really ever go away, even when I did find God's peace. Every time someone else in the family got pregnant, or gave birth, I'd still wish it was me. And as I held their child, I would long for it to be mine. Slowly, I learned to offer to care for their children, their babies, so I could enjoy the experience of being around them, being part of their lives. It was hard, but I knew I needed to do it, partly for the joy I was otherwise denying myself and partly so I wouldn't become bitter. And I did learn to love my sisters' children, in particular—especially Mary. We seemed to have a special relationship. She would show me things she had found, or little things she made. What sweetness to share her pleasure. And she was a spiritual little thing too. She would talk to me about God and ask questions about what her Uncle Zechariah did in the temple.

As I say though, when I really knew I was pregnant, something settled, and I knew every vestige of reproach had gone. God was giving me a child of my own, but obviously giving me a child that was very special, with a special purpose. I knew Zechariah believed that too, and there was a deep expectation within me. Even though I'd believed him that I would get pregnant, I hid it from others. There were too many who wouldn't believe. They would just think I was giving in to old fantasies. And, anyway, it was so precious, I didn't want to share it. It was as though, somehow, it would make cheap this amazing gift growing inside of me. So I kept it hidden, easy enough. I've got a bit of fat on my old bones anyway, and flowing robes cover everything. And I didn't want people to think that I thought I was something special, either: that I was somehow claiming that I deserved God's favor. I knew I didn't. I knew that God knows every inch of my being. So I kept it secret . . . until the day Mary arrived, up from Nazareth. I hadn't seen her since the last Passover visit, and still my family knew nothing. When I realized it was her, hurrying up the hill as though the glory of God was about to burst on her, I knew she would be the first one I'd tell. And then something happened that made it even more significant. I'd been feeling the baby moving within me for a little while already, but only little movements, little kicks I suppose. But as I heard Mary call out in greeting, it was as though the babe did a somersault. I don't suppose he could have really but that's what I imagined! And it felt indeed as though the glory of God had swept in with her. And I found myself saying something I didn't even understand, "Why is this given to me that the Mother of God should come to me?"

We both looked at each other and laughed and held each other, and then both started talking at once: me explaining that I was pregnant, and she saying she knew already; me asking how she could possibly know, and she saying an angel told her. If it had been anyone else saying that, I might have been the one making accusations of fantasies. But I knew, with her it would be the exact truth. And then I told her how my baby had leapt inside me. And then I demanded of her!—why I had said what I did—"The Mother of God," what was that about? Eventually, we slowed down and told the other our stories. And she put her hand on my swelling belly and laughed as the baby kicked some more. The light in her eyes was a marvel. And when she told me she, too, was pregnant, even though she and Joseph weren't even married yet, somehow I knew this was true, though beyond human comprehension. But she was radiant. Some pregnant mothers are. You don't have to even be told—I, who used to be so sensitive about such things, used to notice. But she was beyond even that. It was indeed as though the radiance of God was with her. And she just kept talking about how amazing God is. She started singing from the psalms. But then she just kept going, weaving bits of psalms with her own words. I tried to write some of it down afterwards because it was like a prophecy flowing from her.

> My soul magnifies the Lord, and my spirit rejoices in God my Savior.
> Because he knows how small and undeserving I am, no better than anyone else. And yet now everyone is to be blessed through what he is doing through me!
> The Most High God has done wonderful things for me, the Holy God of our fathers.
> His compassion is poured out on those who know him, and are in awe of him, through all of our ancestors' times and right into ours.

> He has shown how powerful he is by using the poor and the lowly. As he always does!
> And the proud, and the oppressors, and the rulers, and the conquerors—it makes no difference to him.
> It is to us that he comes, the poor, the humble, those who have no claim to anything.
> Those of us who hunger for him, it is to us that he comes. And to those who think they have everything, well they don't need anything more than they have already.
> He hasn't forgotten Israel, and left us to our enemies. It is to us that he comes.
> He has always cared for us. And now, again, he is coming to us in a way they will never guess—a hidden and secret way, bringing salvation through the least. As he always said, to Abraham and all our fathers: He is coming to us.

Mary continued, "Oh Elizabeth, what kind of God is this that would come to our people through being born a baby, through the womb of one such as I? How can it be that the Almighty God has made me pregnant with the holy, bringing to birth his presence through me?"

And what could I say? I did not know what special purpose he had for my child, but I knew it was something special. I didn't know why he had chosen me. I too was pregnant with the holy, and would somehow bring to birth the presence of God. Oh, not in the same way as Mary maybe, but still bringing forth the holy. And what had I done to deserve that? Nothing. I knew it wasn't about deserving. I knew Mary had spoken the truth. This is what our God is like. He delights in using the ones who know they do not deserve. He takes pleasure in satisfying those of us who know we need him, as she said, who hunger for him.

She stayed with me three months, until I was nearly ready to give birth, and she knew without a doubt that she was pregnant. A hard road it will be for her. But she already knew how to find the presence of God to help her through. She knew that that was the only way. She was way ahead of where I was. She knew she deserved nothing, but that those who deserve nothing are the ones the Almighty comes to. And she laughed in delight at the thought.

MARY'S HUMILITY BECOMES MINE

As I identified with this village girl, who could laugh in delight at the thought of being made pregnant by Almighty God, I continued to ponder on the idea that we are all "pregnant with the holy." All of us carry the seed of God within us, and all of us bring to birth the presence of the Creator God—incarnate in each of us in a unique way.

Like Mary, I am deeply humbled by this. And if I follow Mary's way, I receive humility but dance with joy, knowing that nothing I do or have done makes me deserving of the visitation of the Divine Other—only that God chooses to bring to birth something holy from my life.

6

The Older Sister

DIFFERENT PARTS OF ME

Sometimes identifying with a person in a gospel story helps one come face-to-face with another character in a story, one that we might need to acknowledge is also a part of our inner being. We have various traits that are similar to the different characters in a story. I am impulsive, like Peter; I am loving, like John; I am critical, like Judas. Often we identify with a character, and this helps us to process that part of ourselves but frequently it is another character, one we do not want to identify with, who is an important challenge for us.

A Dream Revealing My Shadow

This idea of identifying myself with a less-dominant character occurred to me when I was challenged with the story of the prodigal son (which later led me to find the characteristics of Mary and the Martha within me). I had identified initially, as many of us do, with the prodigal son.[1] I recognized my need to come to the father in repentance,

---

1. Luke 15:11–32.

knowing my need for forgiveness, and I had experienced the father's prodigal love and acceptance with gratitude and joy, especially as there is a part of me that is just as judgmental and critical as the older brother. In my case, of course, it is the prodigal daughter who comes to the father, and it is the older sister part of me that is critical. The older sister part of me, who kept finding fault and kept accusing me, was what created one of the most difficult parts of accepting my marriage break-up. It wasn't until I had dreamed about it that I found a way forward.

In my dream, I was arguing with my real-life older sister in the back of the car. My father told us, "For goodness sake you two, stop arguing." When I recounted the dream to my spiritual director, she suggested to me that I needed to somehow befriend this older sister part of myself. "After all," she said, "God loves the older sister part of you, as well." I found this very challenging. I liked being the prodigal; I desperately needed the grace the father poured out on me as the prodigal daughter. How could I befriend this older sister, who after all refused to come in and join the celebrations. As I reread the story about the prodigal son, I could indeed see the Father's love for the older sister. "Everything I have is yours," he tells her. And I see that the older sister indeed loves the Father, wants to serve him, please him, and do what is right by him. There is no problem in seeing her love for the Father. It is the free grace to the wrongdoer that is the problem.

I struggled with this for days. How do I find the connection between the prodigal daughter and the older sister—both, I had to admit, were parts of me. I would rather reject that self-righteous judgmental part, even though I knew it was also the part of me that held high standards and a great work ethic.

Then one day I found a key. At the time, I had on my computer desktop a painting of the *Annunciation* by Charles Watt. In it, Mary is very young, maybe fourteen. She has her fingers in her mouth and her eyes just looking, as if trying to take it in. She is innocent, young, idealistic. I found myself saying to God, "How could you do that to her? When she is so young." And suddenly, I remembered my sister and myself as teenagers: young, idealistic, wanting to please God with all we knew. And I saw the older sister/brother in the parable as Mary would have been as a teenager, wanting to please her father, wanting to do the right thing by him all her life. And she did so. And I could love her again. This older sister part of me so wanted to please God, and did so by doing the right thing, over and over, by choosing loyalty and sacrifice, and duty, and commitment. This older sister part of me has had to accept the rest of me as needing grace, and I have struggled so much to do so, preferring to come to God on the grounds of doing right. And, instead, I have had to embrace the prodigal part of me who has failed and is in need of forgiveness and grace as the only way back home.

In his story, Jesus doesn't tell us whether the father persuades the older brother to come in or not. The story ends with the father telling the older brother of his appreciation and love for him, and his love for his brother.

These two parts of me have had to learn to get on. The older sister part of me is learning to enjoy the celebration of the prodigal part of me. Sometimes she reverts and wants go and sulk outside and be recognized for her self-righteousness and hard work. I suspect she is like that—I am like that—far more than I want to admit. I suspect my colleagues know this side of me better than I do. I hide my self-righteousness from myself. I hide my judgmental thoughts and criticisms. Or so I think. I suspect my colleagues read far more in my face than I want them to. I want them to think of me as gracious and kind, knowing God's grace and extending it consistently.

But I have been learning to recognize my own shadow[2]—that part of me that I prefer not to see or acknowledge. Many of us think that our "shadow" is actually "sin" and, therefore, we should turn away from it, not acknowledge its existence. But the major part of my shadow is actually good, often a part of me that has a lot of energy and motivation. Maybe a small part of it is self-centered, or "sinful." Maybe it was something we were reproved for as children, or rejected for, and so we turn away from it. In seeing myself in the prodigal son story, I recognized the critical, self-righteous part of me that I do not want to acknowledge. But in trying to befriend this part, I finally remembered the idealistic, committed, hard working, and highly principled teenager. And therefore was able to admit that these are still characteristics I value. The critical, judgmental part was like the tip of an iceberg, but a very valuable iceberg. And that is what a shadow is like: the part we don't like, and try to hide from, is covering qualities and aspirations which are good and valuable. I am not supposed to discard my shadow, indeed I cannot. In the physical world, whenever I am in the light I will have a shadow. In the psychospiritual world, I will always have a shadow. And I am called to befriend it, recognize the good qualities of it. Only then will I be able to live out those good qualities.

2. Johnson, *Owning Your Own Shadow*, 23.

As we recognize our own shadow, the good qualities of it become more a seamless part of ourselves, and the negative qualities are more able to be modified. When we do not recognize our shadow, the positive qualities are hindered. The negative qualities can flare out unexpectedly, or in ways we are not aware of, or they are projected on to other people—that is, either we see the negative qualities in someone else, and take an often unreasonable dislike to that person, or we see the positive qualities in someone and fall in love with them or set them on a pedestal and treat them as if they were god-like.

Identifying with contrasting characters in a story can help us acknowledge the parts of us we turn from, or of which we do not see the value. Often the person in the story we do not easily identify with can represent the shadow part of us. The story of Mary and Martha is a story of an older and younger sister—both representing two parts of me.

THE TWO SISTERS

> ... and a woman named Martha received him into her house. And she had a sister called Mary, who sat at the Lord's feet and listened to his teaching. But Martha was distracted with much serving; and she went to him and said, "Lord, do you not care that my sister has left me to serve alone? Tell her then to help me." But the Lord answered her, "Martha, Martha, you are anxious and troubled about many things, one thing is needful. Mary has chosen the good portion, which will not be taken away from her" (Luke 10: 38b–42).

The Older Sister

∽∽∽

Mary:

Jesus is coming for dinner tonight. I am so happy. I love it when he comes. He opens up the world in ways no one else does. He talks about God as if he was right here with us, not far off in the heavens. He talks as though he's interested in ordinary everyday things, the beautiful little valley lilies, the sparrows, a lost coin, gathering in the wheat, the purple shine on a grape, the crippled boy. And he talks about God as though he knows him. When he gives thanks at the beginning of the meal, I sometimes watch his face and it is as though he is looking right into the face of God. There is this light that comes in his eyes. It touches something in me that I hardly ever let anyone else see. I want to talk to God like that, too. Sometimes I do, when I'm way out on the hillside with no one else around. And sometimes I even feel as though God answers me, like a soft breath of wind against my cheek. I wouldn't tell anyone that though. People don't understand me as it is. I've always been called a daydreamer, the quiet one, the shy one. "Oh, yes, Martha and Mary, the sisters; Mary's the shy one, isn't she?—a bit of a dreamer. I can't imagine her managing a household. Not like Martha does." That's how people talk. And so I've learned not to tell anyone of my dreams, but Jesus. He talks about the things I dream about, as though they are everyday realities. And when people mock him, he just ignores it, or gives them such a look that they shut their mouths. He lives in the world I dream about. And somehow he lives in this one, too. So when he comes—well, I just want to sit and listen to him every minute. It's as though someone else knows this world so precious to me. And he goes further. He imagines it being a world where everyone can live: where we all care for each other, and listen to each other, and love each other. If I said any of that, people would call me a romantic, starry eyed, quixotic. They probably call him that, too, behind his back. But he doesn't seem to care.

If I do everything I can to prepare for the meal before he comes, maybe I can get to stay out of the kitchen for a while. If I keep Martha happy the rest of the day, maybe she will let me beg off the last minute things. I hate to be stuck in the kitchen when Jesus is here talking, and Martha getting bossier every minute. People are right, we are such opposites. She is so capable and competent; she remembers everything and gets everything done—down to the last detail. And, of course, people love coming to our place for dinner because of that. She loves serving them, making sure they get just what they want. And I know she likes what Jesus says, too. Somehow she half listens as she goes in and out. She gets the gist of it, and loves it too, but in a different way. She tries to put what he says into practice. I've seen her try to change the way she talks to people, to care how they're feeling.

But she wants me to be more like her: "Oh Mary, have you still not got that done. What a daydreamer you are. Now go out and get the herbs and don't just stand out there watching the birds . . ." She doesn't understand that sometimes I just have to watch the birds. Well, maybe she does understand, but she thinks it should be after all the work is done.

Martha:

Jesus is coming for dinner tonight. I'm so glad. I love it when he comes. I love seeing Lazarus so animated when they're in conversation. And I love seeing the others with Jesus, too. There's always such a buzz of ideas and discussion and questions. And, of course, others from the village drop by; they join in. They know they're always welcome at my place. They are welcome to come and listen, and to eat with us, too. They know I won't mind, that I will always have cooked extra. I love it when our home can be such a center of activity. I know I sometimes get a bit caught up with it all. I try to cook special dishes, and to do that little bit extra. Sometimes I get a bit bossy in the kitchen, especially with the last minute stuff. I do so like to have everything just so. But that's my gift to all of them: to try and have everything just right, everyone comfortable, everyone well fed. And I love it when everything is cleaned up and put away and we're all relaxing together. Sometimes when I join in at the end, Jesus will turn to me and ask a challenging question. "Now Martha, you've been listening to all this. What do you think?" And I'll say my bit about how I see the kingdom of heaven and how we are to bring it into our lives. And usually he'll nod and I'll know that I've caught what he was talking about. I like the way he challenges. He's such a straight-talker. "Now Martha you didn't listen properly; that's not what I said." Usually it's something I heard perfectly well, but didn't really like for some reason. Like, "Why should I pay someone who's only worked an hour the same as someone who's worked all day in the blazing sun?

That's not justice." "Martha I didn't say it was justice. You don't have to pay them the extra. That's not what I said. I said this is what the Father is like. This is what the kingdom of heaven is like. It goes way beyond justice, into grace." And I'm caught. I know that's what he said. I just didn't like the challenge of it. He gives me a grin and turns to someone else. And there will be Mary, sitting at his feet if she gets half a chance, listening, hardly saying a word, but with such rapt attention, drinking it in. She wouldn't be arguing with him about justice. She'd be flying into grace as fast she could. She'd be giving away all our money to the next beggar, if I'd let her. And the way Jesus looks at her, with such gentle love. She has a special place in his heart. I don't think she knows it, though. Her head's too far away in the clouds; She's trying to understand this God that Jesus talks about, this God who comes to the least, who looks for the broken and the hurting, and who makes a kingdom by winning our hearts. Mary gets it. In a way she always has, even as a little girl. She was always finding the bird with the broken wing, or going down to the village to visit someone who was sick, or out on the hillside just gazing at the clouds. I don't know how she'll live in this tough world though.

Knowing Myself as Both Parts

It is not that I am Mary and know someone else who is a Martha. Or vice versa. It is not "either, or," but "both, and." I am Mary and I am Martha. Probably, I will identify with one of them more than the other, and others looking on will recognize the Mary-part or the Martha-part in me. But I am both of these. If I acknowledge that I am like Mary the least, I will probably not see either her faults or her gifts in me. If I do not acknowledge how like Martha I am, nor will I see Martha's faults, and gifts, in me. By putting myself into one character and then into the other, I give voice to the more hidden part of me. And I look at myself from different angles. I am more able to concede my faults, and also more able to admit to my gifts—knowing they are not consistently present, knowing they are to some extent self-serving. And so, I am able to be more comfortable with the complexity that I am. I am more able to accept the light and the shadow, the mixed motives, and the longings. I am able to accept the God-gifts and my response.

As I continue the story, I come to Jesus' response. It is in the act of bringing myself into the presence of God that I am transformed, each part of me, including the Martha part. What does she hear?

If this were the only story about Martha, we might be tempted to see Jesus as devaluing her, maybe even not liking her, favoring Mary. But the story of John 11 shows him honoring her, trusting her, telling her he is the Resurrection, something he only told very few. In this story, Jesus challenges Martha, but does it with love.

As I get in touch with my Martha self—my busy, hurried, pressured, achieving self, that part that enjoys the doing—I notice the edge of self-pity. Why do I have to be doing all this? (As if anyone has made me, except myself!) And if I'm honest, I hear that edge: God don't you care that I am so busy, so pressured?

THE TWO SISTERS: CONTINUED

Martha:

He looks at me, "Martha. Martha." He says my name twice; he slows me down. It is as if he has taken my face in his hands to still me, so I meet his eyes. I stop and look at him. He goes to the core of it all. You are anxious about many things. Where does that anxiety come from? What are you proving? Who are you proving it to?

And in that moment I know—I'm trying to prove it to myself, and to God, and to anyone else who will see. But, really, I want God to say, "Well done, good and faithful daughter; I am well pleased with you."

And somehow deep within, I have always believed that I have to keep being as busy as I can—do everything possible instead of just the one thing that is needful.

There is only one thing needful, one thing necessary—what does he mean?

Just plain food—not all the extra things I have done?

The one thing—to sit at his feet like Mary?

One thing—how can there be only one thing? He's right—I'm anxious about many.

Maybe let there be one thing right now. And let Mary be Mary.

For that moment, when he said my name, held my eyes, I could believe him.

I really could get all the necessary things done and still have time to look into his face. And that would be enough—enough for you, God, to be well-pleased.

I see the way he is. He is never flustered, even though he has all these people pressing in on him, wanting his time, his advice, his opinion, his touch. And yet there is a stillness in him, no anxiety. He focuses on the one person, the one thing. I wonder if I could learn to do that.

Knowing Myself in Mary

And what of the Mary part of me? Mary sitting at his feet hears, "Mary has chosen the better part, and it will not be taken from her."

THE TWO SISTERS: CONTINUED

Mary:

As I heard Jesus' words, my heart leaped. I was already half standing up knowing I should go and help in the kitchen, do something helpful, something useful, something to prove my time is not being wasted. And this part of me—my heart open to God, close to tears knowing his presence—I will close that down and get on with doing something productive, something others will see and value. And then Jesus gently but clearly cuts across all of that. "Mary is choosing the better thing to do." He is pleased with me! He does not see me as a useless daydreamer. He values my listening, my presence, my attentiveness to him. And it doesn't matter what anyone else says!

I thought I had to do something useful to please him. Is it possible that you would say, "This is my beloved daughter in whom I am well pleased." Just by my sitting here in your presence, this is enough to please you?

There is nothing I have to do to please you, except to be. Accepting your love, your pleasure as a child does, this is what pleases you. A child just is.

ACCEPTING THE PARTS WITHIN

So I learn to value this Mary part of me. This quiet, shy, inner part that so longs for the kingdom: the one who I sometimes push aside for the demands of the "real" world. And I appreciate the older sister part of me also: the part that can see what needs doing and will get up and do it, the part that takes responsibility and does the hard work, even without recognition or thanks. But I try to notice when the older sister part is working too hard, or becoming self righteous and judgmental. I invite her to celebrate the presence of the Beloved, and the presence of the more sensitive parts of myself.

7

Opposites

THE PART I DON'T WANT TO KNOW

As a lecturer, using the Ignatian process with my classes has given me windows into the lives of my students. By focusing on composition of place, I have taught them to imagine themselves inside the story, by randomly choosing to identify with different characters. Recently, as we read in John's gospel the story of the woman taken in adultery, a woman in her late thirties imagined herself as one of the Pharisees. She was shocked at the recognition that she too was a Pharisee. As she identified with the judgmentalism of these men, she realized that she too was very judgmental of people she saw as not measuring up. It was a startling discovery that moved her to want to be more like Jesus in her dealings with people.

As we identify with different people in a story, we may come to someone we feel we don't identify with at all. How could we identify with Herod or Pilate or Judas? In fact, these characters may tell us more about ourselves than the ones we do identify with. The parts of us that we most hide from, the parts we don't even want to acknowledge at all, may help us see the motives or weaknesses that we are hiding from. Engaging with these parts that we hide from can help transform us in a number of ways. First, it is humbling for us to acknowledge that we too have selfish motives or hidden faults. If true humility means being known for who I am, then acknowledging these motives and faults is part of my journey into humility. Second, acknowledging hidden parts of ourselves also causes these parts to loosen control. And third, there is often tremendous energy attached to the parts of ourselves that we repress or deny.

The Part I Consciously Like May Point to My Own Hidden Opposite

I love the story of Mary of Bethany who, when seeing the death of Jesus approaching, pours out hugely expensive perfume on Jesus' feet. As I put myself in Mary's place, identifying with her extravagant, courageous, self-revealing action, I cringe in pain at Judas's criticism. I suspect that there is a Judas part of me that I can learn from.

MARY WHO GIVES, JUDAS WHO WITHHOLDS

> Six days before the Passover, Jesus came to Bethany, where Lazarus was, whom Jesus had raised from the dead. There they made him a supper; Martha served, and Lazarus was one of those at table with him. Mary took a pound of costly ointment of pure nard and anointed the feet of Jesus and wiped his feet with her hair; and the house was filled with the fragrance of the ointment. But Judas Iscariot, one of his disciples

(he who was to betray him), said, "Why was this ointment not sold for three hundred denarii and given to the poor?" This he said, not that he cared for the poor but because he was a thief, and as he had the money box he used to take what was put into it. Jesus said, "Let her alone, let her keep it for the day of my burial. The poor you always have with you, but you do not always have me" (John 12:1–8).

Mary:

Six days before the Passover Jesus came again. I had been getting worried about him. It was already unsafe for him to come when he came and brought Lazarus back to life. And now it was worse. I'd even heard rumors that some people wanted Lazarus dead too, because too many people believed that Jesus really was a miracle worker—that he was the Messiah—and the Pharisee didn't like it. There's talk about him getting murdered.

And apart from all that Jesus himself has been saying that he has to die, I've heard his disciples talking about it, too. Some of them are sure it's some parable, like his others, or some metaphor that they don't understand. They don't want to ask him because he's been so straight with them. And they know they don't understand what he really means.

But I think he means he is going to die. Literally. So often the others don't get it when he says things literally. Blessed are you poor but woe to you rich. They try and change it to make it softer. But he means it. The poor are blessed; you can see it. They are the ones who come flocking to him. Drink in his words. They don't argue over whether he means this or that. They just come, bringing their sick with them, trusting him to heal. And of course he does. And they are blessed; they go home praising God and wanting to know more about the kingdom of heaven. Whereas, the rich people sometimes come and listen. But then they quibble about what he means. They trust in their riches. I can see it. In their hearts they really don't think they need God. So they just do things their way. And they're not blessed. They're not the ones who go home joyful. They're not the ones who hunger more for God.

And even the disciples. I hear them talking. "Yes, but he doesn't really mean you should give away everything." "Well, look what we've given up so we can follow him." "Yes, but we can go back home if we want to." "And what about this dying business?" "He means dying to the ambitions of this world, surely—dying to this world's way of doing things."

But I disagree with them. I think he really means dying. He keeps saying it, with this purposeful look on his face. I can see him trying to get them to understand. It scares me. How can we live without him? We're only just beginning to understand what he says about the kingdom. We'd lose it all if he was killed. How can we live without him? The light he has brought into our lives. The sense of God's reality. God's presence. I can't imagine life without him coming. Oh God, please don't let it come to that. What would my life be like?

Judas said something today, though, that made me wonder. Sometimes Judas gets things that the others don't. He's a sharp one, sometimes too sharp. He's got a critical tongue and can cut people to shreds if he has a mind to. I steer clear of him. But I know Jesus likes him, loves him; I hear the way they talk. Judas has a quick mind. He understands the big picture sometimes; he sees things from a different perspective. If he could only get past that bitter edge he's got. Anyway, the disciples were talking. They were talking about how it will be to go up to the Passover, and whether Jesus can slip into Jerusalem without being noticed. And then Judas set me thinking. He said to them, "But maybe he has to be noticed. He tells us he has to face death. Maybe he's going to face up to them once and for all."

I started thinking about that. Jesus talks about dying. And he talks about resurrection, too. And I of all people know that's possible. I was right there when Lazarus came back to life. I have seen it with my own eyes. But I'm scared. The chief priests are after him. And he's going to Jerusalem. And he says he's going to be delivered up to them and be killed. Then he says he will rise on the third day. Now I'm the one who is asking what he means. But one thing I know: when he talks about it, he is very sorrowful. I feel it in my heart. There's this steadiness in him, as though he knows this is what he must do, but a depth of sorrow too. All the more because we do not understand, he's trying to tell us something deeply significant. I was watching his face today as he talked about it. There's so much sadness. Anguish. He has brought so much love to hundreds of people. Thousands of people have sat and listened to him. And now in this he is so alone, and deeply sad. I wish there was something I could do, some response to make to show something of our love for him. My love for him. My hearing his heart. My longing to comfort him.

I've been thinking about what I might do. I have some nard. I know Martha will think I should keep it for when I'm married. But I want to give it to him. I want to anoint him with it to show my love, to show that we've been hearing him. Tonight after dinner. I know some of them won't understand. I don't care; I want to do it for him. I cannot bear that he would leave us and not know that we hear him and love him more than anything. And all that matters is that he should understand.

I did it! And he understood! That is all that matters—that he understood. He understood what I was doing better than I. I only knew I wanted to respond, to show our deep love for him. Yes, do something extravagant. But he understood. "She did this for my burial," he said. And I would have too, if I was the one burying him; I would have poured this out on his body. But, oh, I am so glad I did it now, now while he is alive and could understand. I still don't know what Martha thought; I did not dare look at her face. I was so afraid she would be angry and see it as a waste. Maybe not though; she's been changing lately. Changing since Jesus gave Lazarus back to us. She's caught something of his depth and something of the other kingdom. But Mary's face I saw. Mary of Magdalene. She understood. I could see it. She would have poured out her very soul for him, would pour out her life blood if it would do any good. I saw her face and knew. But otherwise I was only looking at Jesus. I didn't dare look at anyone else. I so hoped he would understand. I thought he would. I heard about the prostitute washing his feet with her tears, and he defended her. He understood her. And, thank you God of the heavens, he understood me. He knew that I was pouring out my heart as I poured out the nard. He knew I'd caught something of what he was trying to say to us. He saw deep into my secret heart. I've been hurt too many times before to let people see. I try to hide this part of myself. But he looked and saw, and knew what I was saying: saying what words could not express. My heart poured out on his feet. So that if it is to death he must go, he will know he goes with our devotion, our deepest love. I cannot bear that he should go so alone, so misunderstood. But he understood. "She has kept this for my burial," he said. He defended me in front of them all, in front of Judas with his criticism. I cringed when Judas spoke up. But I did not look at him. I could not. I could only look at Jesus in hope he understood. He defended me. He knows my heart. Oh God, go with him. Go with him into this darkness he is facing. And may your love and our love be a light around him. As his is to me. For now my heart is ever held. Held by his love. Because I know he understands. He sees my heart.

Judas:

It's all been going wrong lately. I'm getting more and more sure we're on the wrong track. When I first met Jesus I was sure of him. I don't take to people easily, but he had things worked out. He understood the scriptures and the need for someone to step in. He could see the people were like sheep without a shepherd and they needed leaders, leaders who would have the big picture. The long perspective. And he had that. The kingdom perspective. He saw that the people just couldn't understand, like sheep. And he could see that the religious leaders were in it for themselves, to get the praise of men—all hypocrites. And he chose people like me who could also see that. We used to have deep conversations about it as we walked. I know he enjoyed talking about it to me. I'll say it myself; I'm someone who gets hold of an idea quickly, and I see the whole picture better than others do. I knew it wasn't about overturning the Roman Empire, or fitting in with the religious play actors. It was a whole different kingdom. Sometimes I get irritated with the other disciples. They are so slow sometimes. Not necessarily slow to act. Like Peter— he jumps into the sea to find out if he can walk on water! But slow to understand what Jesus is explaining. They start arguing about who is going to sit on which thrones. It's embarrassing to be around sometimes.

But Jesus, he's been everything I ever hoped for. Although now I'm not so sure; maybe I'm getting a bit disillusioned. But back at the beginning, I really saw he was someone different. I'd been burnt too many times by too many people. I had to fight for my place. I know what it's like to have no money, no food, growing up with no father, trying to look after my brothers and sisters after he was killed. Killed because someone made a stupid mistake about who he was and he got on the wrong side of the Romans. Jesus knows what some of that's like too, having to care for a family with little income. That's why he trusted me with the money. He knew I wouldn't waste it, and that I would see through anyone trying to take advantage of us. He knew I was afraid of being without money too. So he trusted me. I'd have to admit he knew it was a temptation to me, too: to pocket some now and then, just to be on the safe side. But he chose to trust me. He's like that. He will see someone's weakness but trust them anyway. So they will overcome it. And it worked for me, too, until recently, until I've started questioning where we are all going to end up.

All this talk about him dying. He's been saying it for a while. But he's been more and more specific. The others still don't understand. But I've been piecing it together: the Shepherd who lays down his life for his sheep, the sheep before its shearers, dumb, and led to the slaughter. It cannot be that a prophet would die outside Jerusalem. I lay down my life of my own accord. Peter says that if it comes to a fight, he will fight—die if need be. He would, too. And if I was more sure of it all, maybe I would too. But I don't see the point of it if Jesus is going to die. What's the point of us trying to go on if he is not part of it? I wouldn't want to be part of this band without Jesus.

Anyway, I don't believe it will be a fight. He says he will lay down his life himself. Well, if that's what he's going to do, just walk in there and let them take him. I'm not going to be part of that. And what will happen afterwards? I need some kind of alternate plan, some insurance. I'm not going back to having no money, and being on the wrong side of the authorities.

Then last night after dinner Mary poured out all that expensive perfume. What we could have done with that money. I've learned to hold my tongue most of the time. But I was tired, and angry, and these things have been getting to me. "Why wasn't this perfume sold and the money given to the poor? It was worth a year's wages." It was. A year's wages poured out in one act! Yes, devotion I'm sure. But there are more effective ways to further our cause than that. And Jesus took her side, against me, publicly. "Let her alone; let her keep it for the day of my burial." The day of my burial. There it is again. So it's getting really close.

Or maybe I've got it all wrong. Maybe he's going to lay down his life once and for all. And legions of angels will come. And at last everyone will see that what we've been saying all along is true. Finally, they will understand. In that case, we should be helping it happen. I'm so tired of this dodging around, avoiding the confrontation. Let's have it out in the open. He is the Messiah. God's kingdom is come. Let's get on with it. The others can have their quarrels about who will sit on what thrones. The Marys of this world can prepare for death and burial. I'm going to make sure I come out safe either way.

Myself as Judas?

It's much harder to put myself in Judas's place than Mary's. But I can identify with some of it. Imagine how it might have been. And in fact it may have been very different for Judas than I have imagined it. The point is that by putting myself into the story I let myself see the weaknesses in me that could lead in this direction. I too can become alienated from others who don't see what I see. I, too, can give in to false comfort, to addictions caused by loss and longing. I too can be critical and stung by someone in authority not siding with me.

What is Jesus' response to Judas? He sees Mary's act of love for what it is, and he values it. He values her, and he does not allow Judas to devalue her. And he challenges Judas. You can give to the poor any time you want to Judas, is that your real motive? Maybe this was something of Judas's disillusionment with Jesus; he could not handle having his own motives exposed.

Seeing the consistency of Jesus' love, I am sure he loved Judas to the end.[1] He washed his feet at the last supper. He passed him the cup of the new covenant.[2] This is the heart of God demonstrated over and over throughout the Bible and throughout history.

So I put myself in Judas's place as Jesus responds to him. I imagine him reflecting on the interchange between them.

JUDAS WHO WITHHOLDS: CONTINUED

Judas:

What is it like to have my motives exposed like that? I defend myself. Justify myself. Cover up. Go back over old ground about why I have made the decisions I have.

Okay so I acknowledge it. I wanted the money for our use, yes, I admit, for my use even, rather than to give it to the poor. But I can't stand how the rich people waste what poor people need. Yes, what I need, what I want. Can I see it as a way of giving glory to God, valuing something precious to God? That's difficult. I'm angry, I know. Angry with myself for saying anything. Exposing myself like that. I should have known Jesus would defend her. He always does. He always defends the weak. What about me? Would I get defended if I needed it? I'd have to say I would. But I never need it. I keep myself well defended these days. I

1. John 13:1.
2. Luke 22:19–21.

keep people at arm's length. Even Jesus. Would I go and talk to him about it? I would have in the early days. I would have got him aside and talked it through, tried to change my reactions, to be more generous and gracious. But now? He's waiting for me, I know. He gives me opportunities. It's me that draws back. And he lets me. He gives me my own space. He's so committed to us making our own choices. In a way it tears me up inside. I see what he's doing and I admire it. I admire him, still. But I'm not convinced it's working. I have to do things my way.

LETTING THE JUDAS IN ME BE EXPOSED

As I put myself in Judas's shoes, and reflect what it would be like to encounter Jesus in this incident, I can experience, in the midst of my criticism and disillusionment that God's heart is ever towards me. And I can know the part of me that withdraws, hardens myself, holds back, defends, as I imagine that Judas did. It does not excuse Judas. It does not excuse me. We make our own choices. But it helps me see where I can go off track. And it helps me have compassion with others who do so also. In Ladinsky's interpretation of St. Francis, he says "Can true humility and compassion exist in our words and eyes unless we know we too are capable of any act?"[3] There is indeed something truly humbling about recognizing in myself the weaknesses that would lead to betrayal—that would lead to "any act."

---

3. Ladinsky, *Love Poems from God*, 37.

8

A Real Life Experience—and Jesus' Life

LINKING REAL LIFE EXPERIENCES TO JESUS, THE PRESENT ONE

ANOTHER WAY to encounter Jesus is to take our present day experiences and to question his reactions to similar events in his own life. This process will bring together his stories and teaching, with our own experiences. In the story that follows, it was particularly easy to make the links because I was in Israel at the time. Nevertheless, it is always possible to find common ground with my lived experience and with that of his, who "in every respect has been tempted as we are."[1] The question of "What would Jesus do?" comes alive as we find a parallel with our experience and his. The words can be changed to ask what would Jesus have me do, in my present situation, as I walk in a living relationship with him?

Finding Jesus in Bethlehem

This question came alive to me, especially after an incident while visiting Israel. My own experience made me question what life would have been like for Jesus living under Roman oppression, and how he responded to that. In fact, he didn't

1. Heb 4:15.

say much directly about it. But he clearly responded to it. Living in a free country, as I do, I seldom encounter government oppression as millions of people in other countries do daily. And so my encounter with Israeli soldiers while I was amongst Arab people was a challenge for me. The day after this event (described below), I was in Nazareth and meditated on how Jesus, while growing up, may have learned about oppressive power.

ON THE WRONG SIDE OF THE BETHLEHEM CHECKPOINT—(JULY 12, 2006)

The memory of Israel that will probably stay with me the longest is my brief experience of what it is like to be a Palestinian living in Bethlehem today. The first time I went through the Bethlehem checkpoint was in my friend's car. While sometimes passengers have to get out and walk through separately, foreigners are usually waved through easily, as we were on this day. As we drove through the checkpoint this first time, I couldn't help seeing the huge banner as high as the concrete wall saying, *Peace on Earth*. It was put there by the Ministry of Tourism, Israel, for the tourists, I'm sure. But what is most ironic is that the banner is right next to a tower that overlooks the wall that ensures that the inhabitants of Bethlehem (almost all Palestinian: about 40 percent Christian and 60 percent Moslem) stay inside the wall, in a state that can only be called *Peace*, if that means absence of war. It is certainly not the Shalom meaning of peace—a full healthy life—not when there's more than 60 percent unemployment, little freedom to move around the country, and little hope for a better life.

My Own Experience of Oppression

One morning at about seven, I walk out to the checkpoint so I can catch the bus into Jerusalem to meet my cousin for a two day trip to Nazareth and Galilee. As I near the wall, I ask another woman if I was on the right street and so we start walking together. She pauses a moment as she hears noise coming from the checkpoint, and I wonder if there is something wrong. Indeed, once we get there she explains what it was. The checkpoint hadn't been opened. Maybe two hundred men are standing around waiting. Some of them had probably been there since 5 a.m. We thread our way through them, men who were lucky enough to have jobs outside Bethlehem and able to bring back some money to a town which has so little job opportunity. My companion leads me up to the end of the checkpoint waiting area where a number of other women were, near to the other checkpoint where the cars go through. Only cars with yellow number plates are allowed to go through; most belong to Christian or NGO (Non-Government Organization) groups and are let through very easily. The other cars in Bethlehem, those with green number plates, must stay in this West Bank area, where the twenty-foot concrete wall continues to lengthen and make very clear who is in and who is out.

No one knows why the checkpoint isn't open this particular morning; nobody knows when it will open. The women encourage me to go to the car checkpoint saying, "You're a foreigner; they will let you through." So, I squeeze around the barrier and through the wall to the first of the checkpoints. "No," the young soldier says, "no, only cars." "Do you know when it will open?" I ask. "No, you just go back and wait." Another woman comes up. She is pregnant, and a doctor, I later found out. Usually, they let her through so she doesn't have to go through the crush of people at the other pedestrian gate, but not today. When she explains that usually she is let through here, the soldier only replies, "Today is a new day." We walk back to the waiting women and men, who are standing, sitting, and crowded together. The women are sympathetic, but angry. "They just do it to humiliate us." I am inclined to agree. I am a little glad to feel in solidarity with them. I say that I think the soldiers are afraid. "Afraid of what?" asks my companion. Her disbelief reflects the reality that the soldiers have all the power, and they none.

One of the older women tells me she is sick and she is afraid she will be hurt if she has to go through the massing crowd. Usually, they let her through the car check point, too. She yells angrily at a young woman soldier who appears. The soldier yells back. No explanation. No compassion.

A few cars are being let through but any passengers have to come and join the waiting crowd. Another woman is shouting at the soldier. "Where's your captain?" She turns to me, "They should let you through; why don't you ask them for the captain." I reason that I might be able to do more good than the women who are shouting in anger. I go through the crowd again. I ask the young woman soldier this time, "Can you tell us when the gate will open?" "No." "Can I see someone who is over you?" "No." She does not yell at me, but is barely polite. "You must go back and wait." The pregnant woman joins me and says, "But there are so many people, it will take so long to get through." "Look," says the soldier, "they are letting them through now." We see a few men running as they are let through the first turnstile, one at a time. I wonder how often they are late, and how many times of this can happen before they will lose their jobs. It was obviously not a security problem—the cars were waved through easily.

A car comes up and the passenger, a South African man, is sent to join us. He tries to appeal to the soldiers, but to no effect. He tells them he knows someone in a group who monitor such things. He will report them, he says angrily. No effect. He makes his way through the barrier and we chat a little. He says he is doing an internship with the UN. With this experience in Israel, he now realizes what the South Africans did to the blacks. "These are human beings," he says, "and this is apartheid. No wonder they get angry sometimes." He apologizes about his outburst at the soldiers. "I don't usually react like that," he says. I agree that in the countries we are from we are used to cooperation, at least explanation.

I go down and look at the pedestrian gate where the men are massed. I can see through the bars of a second locked gate the crowd of about thirty people crushed together in the small area between wall and turnstile. The few women seemed to be in a line against the wall. The men are allowing the women to join the line even though they have not been waiting as long as the men. They can hardly move in there. Yesterday, when we had climbed a church tower in Jerusalem, my old claustrophobia had returned, and now I feel it again just below the surface, my heart beat increasing. I wonder if I will be able to go through that crush of people, or will I panic at that awful feeling of not being able to move, not being able to get out, with a locked turnstile in front. I turn to my companion, "How long do you think it will take?" "Maybe till ten," she says, "for all this crowd." I wonder if I'll miss the trip to Galilee because I am too afraid to stand in that constricted crowd.

I consider that I could go back and get my friend's car. I could drive it through and park on the other side of the checkpoint. She needs it today, but maybe she could walk through after ten and pick it up. I am grateful that I even have such an alternative. The women are still shouting at the soldiers intermittently, and the huge metal gate where the cars go through begins to close, ignoring the honking of a waiting car. I feel the claustrophobia of being behind the wall, the gate closing. What if you lived here, like these ones, and could never get out? I can't stand the thought. I look through the bars again. Could I handle it?

Suddenly, the South African man appears. "They're letting the foreigners through," he says. I am in tears—of relief and shame. I turn to my companion. She is glad for me, but I am ashamed that I should be given such preferential treatment. "I am so sorry," I say to her as I leave and walk through the car check point where the girl soldier barely looks at our passports. The pregnant doctor is through, too.

We still have to go through a section of the checkpoint. We go through a door and join those who must have been waiting for an hour or two at the gate. We join a line at another turnstile, a simple line of a dozen or so people, not a crush. I am so relieved. The sick woman appears. They must have let her through, too. I greet her as if she were a friend. The men are letting the women go to the front of the line. We wait for the slow permission of the turnstile, locking between each person, sometimes remaining locked, and then turning, often two squeezing in together. I stand in the turnstile waiting with a Moslem woman. A man who is ahead of us steps aside to let me go first. I am humbled by their graciousness. They have waited in line for an hour or two, at least. I skipped the line because I am a foreigner. I then go to the front of the line because I am a woman. And these men, frequently humiliated but still patient, stand aside for us and let us through. These Arab men I would trust more than the soldiers.

Our bags go through a scanner where another soldier sits behind thick glass. We go around the corner. Another line. A girl behind glass is checking papers. Again, I can go through first, my passport barely seen. And then I am out into the fresh morning on the other side. After all, it took less than forty minutes. These people face this arbitrary decision making day after day, without hope of it getting better. The expectation is that it will get worse. I hope I will never have to experience this again. And all I had endured was forty minutes.

Taking It to Jesus' Life

This incident challenged me to reflect on how Jesus might have responded. The next morning when I was sitting on a hillside in Nazareth, I imagined that Jesus too would have risen early here and sat in the quiet of a new day, talking with his Father and preparing his heart for the events of the day. Maybe his events would include nothing more than carpentry work and, no doubt, frequent conversations with people and everyday events and, maybe, occasionally an encounter with a Roman soldier.

I imagine Jesus in the carpenter's shop, working with his father.

IN THE CARPENTER'S SHOP

Joseph and Jesus are trying to finish a job they had promised to someone. Some difficulties had arisen and the whole thing had taken longer than they expected. A Roman soldier comes by and seeing Jesus demands him to carry his satchel. It was the law that he could make such a demand, and Jesus and his father exchange a look as Jesus hoists the bag up on his shoulder. He and the soldier start walking down the long hill, the dust hovering in the air around them. The soldier talks on and off, happy to use the teenager as a slave, but wanting human company, too. Jesus says little, listens, adds a word here and there. They reach the stone that indicates the distance they have walked from the town center; and Jesus is no longer obliged to carry the soldier's bag. The soldier is in the middle of telling some petty story and Jesus keeps walking. The soldier says nothing, happy to have him walk farther, the weight taken for as long as he can. They keep walking for a mile and a half. The soldier begins to get suspicious. What is this Jew playing at? He's not stupid, that's obvious. He must know it's more than a mile. Finally he demands, "Why are you still walking with me? I can only make you walk one mile for me." Jesus smiles—already that smile that has such a depth of knowing. "No," he says, "you couldn't make me walk a mile." "It's the law," says the soldier, "It's part of being under our rule." "I am under another Rule," says Jesus. "And under that Rule I am free. I chose to walk the mile with you. And I am choosing to walk the second."

JESUS' WAY OF BEING—FOR ME, TODAY

Who knows if any such incident as the one above occurred? But I suspect it did because Jesus has such authenticity, he so clearly lives what he speaks, that I wonder if he didn't have experiences like this, which enabled him to say, "If any one forces you to go one mile, go with him two miles. If anyone strikes you on the right cheek, turn to him the other also" (Matt 5:39, 41). How could he say it, unless he himself had done it? And how could he have done it himself unless he had learned along the way, little by little, the truth of his Freedom. He was not a man who lived in occupied territory. He was a man who lived in his father's kingdom, and an earthly territory occupied by others. Freedom is in the heart. And humility is learned through choosing that kind of freedom. It is not freedom to have to strike back when someone hits you. It is not freedom to have to let them pummel you. It is freedom that chooses the response, or the non-response, and knowing the cost.

Jesus, who did not answer the charges laid against him,[2] who did not answer Herod's taunts,[3] who answered to only some of what Pilate said,[4] this Jesus had indeed learned how to respond, or not to answer, according to his own freedom and interaction with God. Jesus lived in another kingdom and recognized another authority.

What if he lived in an oppressed nation today? The inner work is still the same: to find the freedom (and discipline) of interacting with God, to respond to the prompting

2. Matt 27:12.
3. Luke 23:9.
4. Matt 27:14.

of the Spirit within (to obey a higher authority and make that the focus), and to seek first the kingdom of God[5] in a whole new way. Experiencing injustice at the checkpoint and then reflecting on Jesus' words and implicit experience have made me think about it all differently. How would Jesus display social justice? The answer must first come from reflecting on Jesus' responses.

---

5. Matt 6:33.

9

Remembering the Child I Was

COMING TO A STORY FROM A DEEPER LEVEL

Sometimes we hear the gospel stories in church or in some other context. Frequently, the preacher will draw some important point out of the story, or will tell us some theological or historical details to help our understanding. Because I have learned to put myself into the gospel stories, I have learned their meanings at deeper levels and have drawn them into my life in a different form. The stories of people who brought children to Jesus have been the subjects of many sermons. Mostly, the preacher explores what qualities Jesus might have been talking about: humility, innocence, trust, intuitiveness. And all of these qualities may be important, but I suspect if we were to imagine ourselves into the story, we would get closest to the heart of its meaning. Now, I don't imagine what the story might be like, but I remember what it was like for me when I was a child, for instance, and then I imagine that child—myself—in the story.

> And they were bringing children to him, that he might touch them; and the disciples rebuked them. But when Jesus saw it he was indignant, and said to them, "Let the children come to me,

> do not hinder them; for to such belongs the kingdom of God. Truly I say to you, whoever does not receive the kingdom of God like a child shall not enter it." And he took them in his arms and blessed them, laying his hands upon them (Mark 10:13-16).

Also, in another incident:

> And calling to him a child, he put him in the midst of them, and said, "Truly, I say to you, unless you turn and become like children, you will never enter the kingdom of heaven. Whoever humbles himself like this child, he is the greatest in the kingdom of heaven" (Matt 18:2-4).

Myself as a Child

What strong words these are! How can I best understand them? I try to remember the child I was. When I was about eight years old I went forward at a big public meeting in response to a gospel appeal. I had already given my life to Jesus, at home with my mother. But I felt sure that God was asking me to do it publicly, during the singing of a hymn of consecration. I plucked up courage and did it. Out in the back of the meeting room, being "counseled," and signing a "confession of faith," I overheard one of the women saying, "She's too young to know what she is doing." I think my mother was there and she defended me. I don't think I said anything. But inside, I knew that I knew what I was doing. As I read the stories of Jesus and the children again, my guess is that my childish perception of what I was doing was closer to what Jesus wanted than the grownups' perceptions were.

I am to "receive the kingdom of God like a child." As I try to put myself back in my child's skin, I am struck with how hopeful, how possible everything is, even a bit magical. I wanted to be a missionary, and read missionary stories from quite a young age. Time, then, had a different quality. I remember when two weeks' school holidays felt as though they would go on forever. I was able to stay in the present moment: playing on the beach in the summer; putting fingers gently among the tentacles of a sea anemone to feel the suction; going sailing with my father, and trusting the wind and the sea, and his skill, without thinking about it. And at Christmas, all of us are opening presents as a family, sitting on our parents' bed; sitting around the fire with my father telling stories, eating Saturday night roast dinner, my father reading stories to us over dinner. I embraced the sense of a warm family circle and acceptance. There was nothing to prove. I lived in part of the kingdom, just by being.

I was by no means a perfect child. I remember arguments, and feeling rejected, and saying hurtful words, and feeling alone. Of course. But these did not hinder me from "receiving the kingdom." I believed there was another world, and that God was good, and that living the best I can is what I am called to do.

There is a key here. I, as an adult, am called to get in touch with the child I was, to remember and re-envision that wide-eyed hope for a better world, where God is sovereign and all is well. I am to do it from the inside—from the inside of the child I was, not as an adult trying to be a child.

I imagine myself as a child standing at my mother's knee as we are preparing to make something, sewing or knitting. She is sitting, patient. I am jiggling with excitement, easily distracted, with the sense of her warmth and willingness ready to go at my pace.

I remember standing in church with my father. It's Easter, and it must be Easter Sunday because we are singing, "Low in the grave he lay . . ." I remember singing it to myself as I walked home from school.

The reality of the kingdom, it is as natural to be part of it as it is to be a part of this world.

MEETING JESUS AS A CHILD

"And they were bringing children to him that he might touch them" (Mark 10:13).

There is a whole group of us, my mother and some other mothers excitedly talking as we walk to this event down on the lake shore. This special man we are going to see. And maybe little Micah will get healed of the sores that he always has up and down his legs. And some of the others are running around, and jumping and racing each other. I hold my mother's hand and skip along beside her. My sister is holding her other hand, walking more quietly. I'm half listening to the grownups' conversation as I watch the others. They are talking about the things Jesus has done, the healings that have happened. And we are going to see him! I'm excited, happy. And there we can see a crowd of people milling around down on the shore. People are coming and going. They are shouting out to each other. There are small groups standing and chatting. It is a bit like going down to the markets. But there's this central group. That's where we are heading for: the biggest group, with a bit of a line waiting. There are some sick people. And somewhere in the middle of that group is this Jesus we've come to see . . .

We get to the line and join in. The other kids are playing a game of tagging, yelling at each other. Everyone's happy. Expectant.

Then some men come along. They ask what the kids are doing and what we want there. One of the mothers tells him. We've just brought the children to him so he can bless them. You know, protect them from evil, and help them grow into good kids. There's a bit of a silence. The men talk among themselves. I don't know what's happening, but it seems to have gone quiet. And then one of the men says, "No, really, there are too many people. There are people with real needs waiting, look there's a blind man." I look where he's pointing; yes, I can see his eyes even from here. "And there's crippled people." Again I look: bandages and sticks. "They're the ones Jesus needs to see. No, he doesn't need to have to bless every child as well. No, you best go home." The mothers are quiet. One tries to argue. Not my mother, though. We turn away. I look up at her face. She's sad I can see. I'm sad, too. I look across at my sister; tears are running down her face. We wanted to see this man. They said he was special, that he would help us know God. I'm disappointed. I drag my feet in the pebbles as we walk away.

Then I hear the woman who was arguing; she yells after us. "Hey, he wants us to come!" My mother keeps walking, not wanting to make any trouble. I look back and see the others all heading back to Jesus. "Please, Mummy," I beg her. She looks down at our faces, my sister still in tears. "We'll see," she says as she slowly turns back. And then I see a man standing up from the beach a little and he's waving to the children, and to us; I'm sure it's to us too. "See, he wants us to come," I say, pulling on my mother's hand. "I think you're right," she says a little hesitantly. But as we see the others gathering around, we hurry to catch up, not wanting to be left out, not wanting the men to change their minds.

But we need not have worried. Jesus is telling them very clearly how important we are. The most important, he says. Then Jesus reaches out to me and I feel as though I've known him all my life. I let go of my mother's hand and go to him. He takes me up on one knee, and my sister on the other. I look across at her. She's just staring up at him with this quiet smile on her face and her eyes wide. He sits there in the midst of all these important grownups talking about us. I feel a bit self-conscious, but important. Jesus is saying something important and special about me. And they are all looking and trying to understand. I don't even have to understand. I just am. That is enough. I snuggle into Jesus, knowing I'm approved of. I'm in the kingdom. Because I know God is. And he loves me. And that is enough.

THE CHILD WITHIN KNOWS IN ANOTHER WAY

As I remember and imagine, I am much more in touch with the simplicity of being in the kingdom as a child. And I am reminded of being able to be myself in Jesus' arms without having to deserve or do anything. The patterns of achieving, and performing, and seeking approval I get hooked into as an adult are about the false self, not the kingdom. The child who I was reminds me . . .

10

Responding to Art

ART SPEAKS TO US IN ANOTHER WAY

Through the centuries, art has been used to help us come closer to the realities and the meanings of the gospel stories. For millions of people through history and in different non-literate cultures, art has been the main means by which people engage with their sacred texts and spiritual stories. Drama, dance, painting, stained glass windows, icons, and songs, all can represent a story or person, which helps us meditate and interact with the Divine.

Each artwork is an interpretation. Artists bring their own histories, preferences, and emotions to the story or character they represent. So when we come to that artwork, we can allow their interpretation to broaden our own interpretation, to question it or to clarify it. We do not have to like the artwork or agree with the interpretation because, whatever the interpretation, it brings an implicit question: How do I understand this story? How does this story speak to my heart? How would I paint it, sing it, dance it?

Henri Nouwen has written a book, all of which is a reflection on Rembrandt's painting of the prodigal son.[1]

1. Rembrandt, *Return of the Prodigal Son,*. c. 1662, Oil on canvas The Hermitage, St. Petersburg.

The Return of the Prodigal[2] is Nouwen's recounting of the hours he spent in front of the picture, allowing it to engage his heart and bring transformation. Of course, he identifies with the prodigal son, who is in his father's loving embrace. And the painting helps him stay with that. However a friend pointed out to him that in fact the life he had lived was more like the older brother, staying in right-standing with his father. He meditates on the brother, looking on in criticism and lack of understanding. Finally, he realizes that he too is called to be the father, to interpret God's love to others. He meditates on the father in the painting, the loving response to the son, the masculine and feminine represented in his hands, the cloak of redemption about him. Nouwen allowed Rembrandt's painting to expand his understanding and his heart.

Rediscovering the Familiar through Art

There are many paintings available to us.[3] The internet is a huge resource. The example I have used as a source of meditation is a painting that is available on the Internet. It is by Lucas Cranach the Younger (1515–1586) and is called *Christ and the Woman Taken in Adultery*.[4] (The original is oil on canvas, and is found in The Hermitage, St. Petersburg, Russia.)

---

2. Nouwen, *Return of the Prodigal Son*.

3. For further examples of using artwork, see Juliet Benner's articles in *Conversations: A Forum for Authentic Transformation* and her book *Contemplative Vision: A Guide to Christian Art and Prayer*, IVP. 2011.

4. Cranach, *Christ and the Woman Taken in Adultery*, c.1532, Oil on canvas The Hermitage, St. Petersburg.

The scribes and the Pharisees brought a woman who had been caught in adultery, and placing her in the midst they said to him, "Teacher, this woman has been caught in the act of adultery. Now in the law Moses commanded us to stone such. What do you say about her?" This they said to test him, that they might have some charge to bring against him. Jesus bent down and wrote with his finger on the ground. And as they continued to ask him, he stood up and said to them, "Let him who is without sin among you be the first to throw a stone at her." And once more he bent down and wrote with his finger on the ground. But when they heard it, they went away one by one, beginning with the eldest, and Jesus was left alone with the woman standing before him. Jesus looked up and said to her, "Woman, where are they? Has no one condemned you?" She said, "No one, Lord." And Jesus said, "Neither do I condemn you; go, and do not sin again" (John 8:3–11).

RECEIVING THE STORY THROUGH THE PAINTING

The painting is a close-up view of Jesus and the woman standing in the center with thirteen men taking up the rest of the picture, presumably scribes, Pharisees, soldiers, and disciples. The men's expressions vary. One man, who I assume is Peter, has his eyes down, seeming to listen attentively to Jesus. A couple of other disciples with him are looking at Jesus, as if trying to understand the import of what he is saying. This is in contrast to others, presumably the religious leaders who are attentive in a different way. The most obvious one, standing to Jesus' right is in conversation with him, his hands raised as if in argument and accusation. Indeed, he looks learned, and critical and judgmental. Jesus stands between him and the woman as if shielding her. The other man in the forefront of the picture is a soldier. In one hand is his helmet filled with large stones. In his other hand is a stone, ready to be thrown; but yet his hand is relaxed, waiting. On his face is a leer, a look partly of lascivious interest and partly of expectant retribution. This look is repeated in other faces. Men ready to condemn what they are aroused by.

In the middle of this cross section of society stands Jesus, quiet, self contained, protecting the woman. His robe is red, the color of redemption. His right hand, as if in answer to the Pharisee's accusing ones, is pointed towards the woman in a symbol of blessing. This is the center of the picture: an open hand, blessing.

The woman herself is almost leaning on Jesus' shoulder. Her eyes are downcast. Her face is demure. She does not look afraid, but simply trusting. In fact, she looks as though she is taking no part in the interchange between Jesus and the Pharisees; she is oblivious to the other men gathered around. And the reason for this composure is seen in the part of the picture that speaks to me most deeply. She and Jesus are holding hands. There in the front, at the bottom of the picture are their hands, her fingers interlaced with his. One's eyes move from Jesus' face and right hand to her face, over her belly (is she pregnant?—the evidence of her adultery?), to their hands. Intimate. She is safe. He will die rather than let them have her, but not in a violent confrontation, simply in quiet defense, holding a standard of righteousness and grace that no one can answer to. She stands quietly trusting.

I wonder about her story. Some have suggested she could have been a prostitute, dragged before Jesus, simply as an object to use, in order to accuse him, to bring a charge against him. And indeed she may have been. But that is not how Cranach has painted her.

To my eyes, he has painted her as modest, middle class, gentle. I imagine a story that could explain her behavior, a story that I can identify with. Perhaps she has been married off to a rich, elderly widower who simply wants an heir and a young wife to comfort him in his older years. Perhaps she has met again the love of her youth, returned after years of exile, and been slowly drawn into a love affair with him, fearing to lose him a second time. Maybe she has been followed by a jealous servant, watching for a chance to accuse her of betraying his master.[5] What reason would have caused her to have risked her life? And what would it be like to be dragged through the streets, publicly shamed for her behavior? How would it be to face death . . . and then look into the eyes of this man who rescues her and refuses to condemn her? And then what life will she lead afterwards? And then she will later discover what it costs him to have taken this stand.

THE INVITATION TO ME TO RE-CREATE

Exploring how Cranach has painted this woman, I wonder how I would have painted her. I imagine her thrown down

---

5. I have explored this possibility in Alexander, *Dancing with God*, 1–7.

in the midst of these men, her hair covering her face, waiting for the stones, and a slow painful death. I see all sandals and boots, and a half-naked woman, her long hair loose, her sin evident.

I imagine Jesus kneeling down beside her, making them all change their position, leaning in to see what he is doing, questioning what is happening. The dynamics of accusation and confrontation is undermined. There is a silence that spreads through the crowd, an uneasiness running through them. There is a slow realization that he has turned the tables; they cannot stand up to him, even as he kneels in the dust. He, indeed, brings into question their understanding of law, authority, and retribution. (I imagine him kneeling in the dust on another day, a crown of thorns about his head, dust and sweat, and a wooden cross on his bloodied shoulders.)

Or I imagine just the two of them left alone, she standing, waiting, disbelieving what has happened, and he still kneeling, looking up at her face, asking her if anyone condemns her. With a look of amazement, she says, "No one, Lord." He says, "Neither do I." I let his answer soak into my soul.

11

Copying the Pattern

USING OTHER STORIES

PAUL TELLS us that all scripture is profitable for teaching.[1] While I have mostly used gospel stories, because meeting Jesus in them is so direct, other scripture stories enable us to identify with very human characters who wrestle with the same issues as we do, question God as we do, and long to know him, like us.

Experimenting

I stumbled on another way to use a scriptural story one day when I was facing the pain of losses in my life. Mostly, I intentionally use gospel stories because they so directly bring me into an encounter with the living Jesus. But I've tried using a psalm, putting my own name into it or simply praying the words as though it is me who is speaking as the original writer did. Or, similarly, I have used the wisdom writing, Song of Songs, or a parable. To do this, I have simply utilized the framework to write my own story. In this next example, I have used the story of Job as it is such

1. 2 Tim 3:16.

a profound story of loss and silence—and, at last, God's response. I used it, also, as I was struck one day with how God's answer confirmed the powerful healing of meditating on creation, far more powerful than arguing about theology and propositions.

THE FRAMEWORK OF JOB'S STORY

The framework of Job's story is like this.

Recounting Job's story

- The riches—his "goodness," all he has and is.
- The losses.
- The basic temptation to give up faith.
- The accusing voices. While these may come from outside of us, the ones that are the most powerful are those that are within us, or where in some way we agree with the external accusations.
- The replies to the voices. The story of Job is a long saga of accusing voices and Job's defenses.
- Then, finally, the call of God to beauty and creation because God does not join in the argument. The accusations and defenses are arguing over the wrong questions.
- And the outcome—seeing God in an intimate relationship, not just hearing about him.

So I tell my story as a contemporary version of Job. I name the losses. I repeat the accusations, the true accusations of my own mind. I articulate my answers to the accusations, answers that are never enough. And at last I listen to God's voice, a voice that does not answer the accusations but that calls me to beauty, and peace, and acknowledgement of a greater knowing.

My Story Retold Following Job's Pattern

Once upon a time there was a woman who had tried to please God since childhood. She read her Bible and went to church and chose a career in missions. She got an education, joined a missionary organization, and married a fellow trainee. She had children and developed a successful career.

Negative voices within her said, "But your intentions are not perfect, you are not good enough."

And over the years came losses.

She lost her father in her early twenties. She left her family to be a missionary. Years later, her husband wanted to leave missions; he wanted to leave her home country to which they had returned. Her children grew up and left, her marriage failed. She lost her home and dreams of community. And her understanding of her faith changed, and some close to her judged that she was no longer a believer.

Some voices said to her, "Why are you a Christian anyway?" and "Are you a really a believer?" But these troubled her little because God was the center of her life.

But other voices cut deeper. And the accusations that were the worst were her own.

"You are not pleasing God because you have not kept your marriage vows—your vows that said for better, for worse, for richer, for poorer, in sickness and health until death parts us."

And she said, "I tried everything I knew. I went to others for advice and counseling. I supported him in all he did, earned an income so he could stay in ministry. I tried all I knew, until I believed it was destructive to both of us."

And the accusing voices said, "That is not good enough. You have to stay till death."

"You are not pleasing God because you are not a good mother; you did not create a good family home; and now your children do not have a home; you did not give them extended family."

And she said, "I tried all I knew to be a good mother, I took them into missions believing that was the best I could give them, I tried to be always there for them."

And the accusing voices said, "You were not a perfect mother. Look at the other families, the family centers they have made, the extended network. You are not pleasing God because you are not, and never have been, a real missionary, even though you said that's what you wanted."

And she said, "I have come to see that mission work is discipling a nation, and I have put myself into that with all I have."

And the accusing voices said, "That is not good enough. You live in a comfortable country, with a good income. You are not in a third world country. You are not pleasing God because you do not live in community nor are you active in church community."

And she said, "I have so wanted it. I try to create community in all my relationships."

And the accusing voices said, "That is not the same thing. That is not good enough. You are not pleasing God because some of your colleagues disagree with you." Your theology is obviously too different. Your ideas are a mismatch."

And she said, "In all that I do I try to understand the kingdom, and how God would have us relate."

And the accusing voices said, "If your life was good enough, then they would be persuaded by that. You are not good enough."

And she said, "Oh God, you alone know my heart. What shall I do?"

God said, "Come away with me, and sit under the pines for hours at a time, and look at the beauty of my world—the mountains and the water."

She said, "And what of these accusations?"

"Sit in the presence of my love, intentionally, over and over every day. And speak to yourself gently and reverently," said God.

She said, "I can only believe that my desire to please you does in fact please you?"

And God said, "Let us make a beautiful patchwork together, of the broken pieces of your life."

And she said, "What of the sins, and the illusions, and the lost dreams?"

And God said, "You and I together will create something beautiful."

She said, "Your love and your grace are enough. You are enough for me."

MERTON NAMES THE DESIRE TO PLEASE GOD AS ENOUGH

My Lord God, I have no idea where I am going. I do not see the road ahead of me. I cannot know for certain where it will end. Nor do I really know myself, and the fact that I think I am following your will does not mean that I am actually doing so. But I believe that the desire to please you does in fact please you. And I hope I have that desire in all that I am doing. I hope that I will never do anything apart from that desire. And I know that if I do this you will lead me by the right road though I may know nothing about it. Therefore I will trust you always though I may seem to be lost and in the shadow of death. I will not fear, for you are ever with me, and you will never leave me to face my perils alone.[2]

---

2. Merton, *Thoughts in Solitude*, 79.

12

Discerning Both Sides—in Me

PERFECTION OR ACCEPTANCE?

I'M SURE that many of us, especially in the first half of life, pray to be made like Jesus, and then imagine that that means being perfect, without darkness, without sin, even without mistakes. If this is our theology, even subconsciously, we will try to deny the parts of ourselves that are imperfect, immature, or unwhole. We may even hate parts of ourselves, instead of learning to listen to inner wisdom that those parts may bring us.

Finding Both Sides Within

In chapters six and seven, two different characters represented different parts of me. It may be more challenging to recognize the two voices from one person. In this next story, the two different parts are clearly seen in the same character. How do I recognize when I am coming from different parts of myself? I am grateful to Peter for his extroversion, his demonstrating how hearing God's revelation is so closely enmeshed with hearing other voices.

> He said to them, "But who do you say that I am?" Simon Peter replied, "You are the Christ, the Son of the living God." And Jesus answered him, "Blessed are you, Simon Bar-Jonah! For flesh and blood has not revealed this to you, but my Father who is in heaven . . . Then he strictly charged the disciples to tell no one that he was the Christ. From that time on Jesus began to show his disciples that he must go to Jerusalem and suffer many things from the elders and chief priests and scribes, and be killed, and on the third day be raised. And Peter took him and began to rebuke him saying, "God forbid, Lord! This shall never happen to you!" He turned and said to Peter, "Get behind me, Satan! For you are a hindrance to me; for you are not on the side of God, but of men (Matt 16:15–17, 20–23).

I imagine myself as Peter trying to sift through the events of the day:

TRYING TO LEARN GOD'S PRESENCE

Peter:

What a day. Well, nearly every day with Jesus has its surprises, but today went from one extreme to the other. Often enough I get rebuked by Jesus. I'm such a big mouth that I'm forever saying things I shouldn't. But then I'm the one that learns: I say things, do things, try things and Jesus lets me know when I'm out of line. But today was about as bad as it can get. It didn't start off like that. And maybe that was why it was so bad when it happened, because I was on a real high from his praise.

Jesus had asked us who people thought he was, in that way of questioning he has that you know is going to lead to something challenging. So we told him what we'd heard. Some say Elijah, some say one of the prophets. People have been saying John the Baptist, all sorts of things. When we'd said all of that, it went a bit quiet. We waited to see where he was going with it. And sure enough, "But who do you say that I am?" he asked. Well I knew what I wanted to say straight off. The Messiah. The Christ. The son of Almighty God. In some ways we had been saying it for a while. In fact it's what Andrew said when he'd first met Jesus and came to tell me about it. I remember, "We've found the Messiah," he said. But it's one thing to say it when everything's new and anything is possible and another to say it when you're in the thick of it; you know it means committing your life to it, and whatever that brings, forever.

Anyway, I said it. And it was as though I was prophesying, speaking out words of truth from deep within me. And even as I was saying it, I felt almost an ache in my heart, like I was saying something that my whole being wanted to grab ahold of. It was like I wanted to sing or shout, that feeling I get sometimes when I talk to people and know that God loves them, wants to heal them; and it makes me love them, too.

Jesus' response was even stronger than all of that, but confirming it too. "Blessed are you, Simon Bar-Jonah! For flesh and blood has not revealed this to you, but my Father who is in heaven."[1] I felt really good. And then he said more about how this was the foundation of people coming together, and how I was part of that. You can imagine I felt like

1. Matt 16:17.

I was on a real high, a real flow of God's Spirit. Maybe that's why I reacted how I did when he kept talking. He started talking about how he would suffer from the religious leaders. I mean we'd just really caught hold of this—he really was the Messiah; this is "kingdom come"; we're going to change everything, bring healing, life, a whole new way of living! And then he said he was going to suffer and get killed. Well there's no way any of us will let that happen, especially not now. Now that we know he's the Christ. But he doesn't want us to tell people. I don't understand it. In one breath he's saying that God says he's the Messiah, but we're not to tell, and they're going to kill him. But then it got worse. I tried to tell him, tried to say that this wouldn't happen. And he turned to me, just after he'd said how God was with me, and rebuked me like he never had before. He called me Satan. I couldn't believe it. I didn't know what to say. I just stood there dumbfounded. "Get behind me Satan."

So I'm trying to figure it out. If he saw Satan in what I said—what did I say, did I feel any different from when I felt like I was prophesying? I said, "God forbid, this will never happen to you." And yes, I have to admit I was rushing in again, wanting to protect him, protect us, protect this wonderful sense of purpose and vision I'd just glimpsed. Hmm. I can see I was kind of taking it all on myself to make it all happen. I've done that often enough. But I think it went further, too. There was more in it than that, fear, I'd have to say, when he talks about getting killed. Well, yes, I know some of the Pharisees are angry and could stir that up, but then we're all in danger. Yes, I'd have to say fear was part of it, and more. He said something more: "You're on the side of men, not of God." So I tried to speak for God. It felt so good, the things that had just happened, and I suppose

I was trying to believe I was still speaking for God. "God forbid." I said that. I know Jesus gets angry when people act like they're speaking for God and they're not. He hates for God to be misrepresented. I suppose I was doing that, acting like I knew what God wanted when I was really only saying what I wanted to say. But there was more to it, too. "You're on the side of men . . ." I think this is the core of it. I went for the way of success. He's the Christ, so let's go out there and impress everyone. There it is again—so clear—my preference to succeed, to look good, to win people by winning. It reminds me. He told us once about the time he had been in the wilderness, and how he was tempted to throw himself off the temple so God could save him and everyone would be impressed with him. I guess if it had been me, I would have said yes. I want people to look at me and be impressed. I guess I thought that he being the Christ meant we could do that now.

Jesus was telling me loud and clear that that is not the way. That's the way of men, that's the temptations of the devil. It's not God's way. Oh God, work this into me. Will I ever learn it?

LIKE PETER, I TRY TO DISENTANGLE THE HOLY AND THE DESTRUCTIVE

So, I find myself in Peter. Some of the time, I really flow with God's Spirit, and know the joy, and the life, and the sense of God's presence that comes with that. Then sometimes I can turn into the darkness within myself: fear, or the desire to look good, or to impress. I have to say I agree with Peter: Oh God, will I ever learn it? Yet, I know too I am learning to discern when I am coming from God's Spirit and when I am not.

It reminds me of the poem "The Two Trees" by William Butler Yeats.[2] He describes the life that flows within us as the holy tree:

> Beloved, gaze in thine own heart
> The holy tree is growing there;
> From joy the holy branches start . . .

As I meditate on this I see how it fits with Peter's sense of God's presence, and the sense of life I have when I am aligning myself with that. But then Yeats contrasts it to the bitter tree that we sometimes turn to:

> Gaze no more in the bitter glass . . .
> For there a fatal image grows . . .
> Broken boughs and blackened leaves,
> For all things turn to barrenness
> In the dim glass the demons hold.

I am conscious of how I can be destructive to myself, how I can interpret people's actions as rejection and so reject myself, and speak cuttingly to myself instead of with God's voice of love and grace.

---

2. Krans, *William Butler Yeats*, 97.

13

To Be Like Jesus

IMAGINING OURSELVES AS JESUS?

Over the years that I have been using this process in my classes, I have found that people seldom choose to imagine themselves as Jesus. Even though we know we are called to be like Jesus, to imitate him as Paul says he does, I sometimes wonder if we find it somehow sacrilegious to put ourselves in his place. Yet surely if we are to be like him, to imagine ourselves in his skin would be a profound learning experience. As long as we continue to focus on Jesus as divine, we will not really believe that he found a way to be human in this world. We will think of his temptations as not really tempting because, "after all, he was God." So, we will miss learning how to draw on God's Spirit, as Jesus did.

A Very Human Jesus—Like Me

As a woman, I don't find it difficult to imagine myself in the place of various men in the gospel stories. I can imagine myself into most stories; I find a point of identification. But I sometimes find it difficult to imagine myself as Jesus, emphasizing his "God-ness," rather than focusing on the reality that he was fully human. He "in every respect has been tempted as we are."[1] He was tired, hungry, thirsty, compassionate, angry, disappointed, grieving, and delighted. I suspect that my hesitation in imagining myself in his place is because part of me holds back from believing that he experienced the world as I do, that he had similar reactions, feelings, hurts, memories. "He learned obedience through what he suffered."[2] Surely, that means he learned how to walk in God's presence by having just those same reactions as I do—and bringing them to the Father. I wonder if putting myself in his place more often will help me understand more how he sees the world, and so help me become more like him. I take up the story of Peter's rebuking Jesus, and imagine Jesus reflecting and remembering.

> Then Jesus was led up by the Spirit into the wilderness to be tempted by the devil. And he fasted forty days and forty nights, and afterward he was hungry. And the tempter came and said to him, "If you are the Son of God, command these stones to become loaves of bread." But he answered, "It is written, 'Man shall not live by bread alone, but by every word that proceeds from the mouth of God.'" Then the devil took him to the holy city, and set him on the pinnacle of the temple, and said to him, "If you are the Son of God, throw yourself down; for it is written, 'He will give his angels charge of you,' and 'On their hands they will bear you up, lest you strike your foot against a stone.'" Jesus said to him, "Again it is written, 'You shall not tempt the Lord your God.'" Again,

1. Heb 4:15.
2. Heb 5:8.

the devil took him to a very high mountain, and showed him all the kingdoms of the world and the glory of them; and he said to him, "All these I will give you, if you will fall down and worship me." Then Jesus said to him, "Begone, Satan! For it is written, 'You shall worship the Lord your God and him only shall you serve.'" Then the devil left him, and behold, angels came and ministered to him (Matt 4:1–11).

JESUS, TRULY IN THE WORLD

Jesus:

When Peter said "God forbid! This shall never happen to you," I was indeed reminded of the temptations in the wilderness. I knew that my Father wanted me to spend time alone with him after John had baptized me. I sensed the Spirit in me, urging me to go without food and to be alone, and that in doing so I would find the ways to stay in my Father's presence. And truly I would learn how to find the ways by finding my own weakest points and turning them to my Father. So, I went out where I would meet no one and could not be distracted from this inner work. The devil, the tempter, the accuser, indeed seeks our weaknesses and tries to play on them. There is nothing like silence and fasting to bring these things to the surface. Of course, I already had spent much time alone with my Father. My habit of getting up early and sitting in creation was something I had learned young and continued through my life. I knew what it was to sit in silence before the day begins, and to know the Spirit of God within who helps prepare me for the day and strengthen my spirit. But the silence over a longer time hollowed out deeper places.

The places where I am most likely to be hooked by the taunts of the enemy became evident. "If you are the son of God," Satan had said. The most frequent accusation I received from people is that I am not who I believe myself to be. It is the same accusation I have heard through my entire ministry, and will no doubt hear to the very end: "if you are the child of the Father; if you are who you say you are; if you really are in relationship with God; if the good you think of yourself is really true." This is the accusation that brings into question my deepest, most precious sense of who I am. It suggests I am less. It implies I am not worthy to be called God's son. It insinuates I cannot live out of this truth. This temptation underlies all the others—is present in the others. As I have learned to live in the presence of the Father, the presence of his love, knowing myself to be his beloved Child, then I am who I am.

After this initial general accusation, the temptations became more specific. I was hungry. I was alone. I was aware of my needs. The first temptation was to make these needs my focus: to look after myself alone; to focus on my needs in this world, as though that is all that matters; to live as if I were one of the privileged ones, who does not need to go hungry, who always has shelter, and comfort, and security; to use any power I have to look after myself and my needs. Again, a temptation I have faced many times since: when we have been hungry, and when the crowds are pressing on us. "Send them away," say my friends, as though it is our needs that matter most. Or when I met the Samaritan woman by the well and needed a drink. I asked her, and we could have left the conversation there, my own need fulfilled. But her need for life was so evident. Or indeed the many times I could have chosen to settle down in one of the seaside towns and enjoy a comfortable life of teaching and healing the few who came my way. But it is my Father's kingdom that is the focus of my life—at whatever cost in physical comfort and safety.

The next temptation was the one Peter remembered, and realized he had aligned himself with: the temptation to impress. He wanted me to draw people's praise and admiration; to attract by success; to choose the way of accomplishment and achievement; and to protect myself from loss, and failure, and rejection. He wanted me to make my decisions based on triumphs and people's approval. Choosing for the kingdom is not the path of popularity and reputation. And when it occasionally does win praise and acclamation, then it is the more subtle temptation, to stay in that place. Living in the kingdom is living with the victories and the losses, and to know the Father's approval as the only approval worth having. I wish to look to his eyes as an indication of the way forward, and not to the eyes of men. Peter had slipped into the world's way—the approval of men—just when he had been so open to hearing the Father's voice. He had recognized the Christ-calling, but then showed he had so little understanding of what it meant. He thought that gave permission to choose the way of glory, of winning people over by feeding their desire for success and esteem. No, we walk the way of descent, the way of surrender, the slow way of humility and trust. We walk the way of living through dying, resurrection through letting go of life. I saw Peter's words as the temptation they were because I had faced this in myself before. I had faced it in the aloneness of the wilderness, where anything was possible. But only God's way was the way forward.

Then the third temptation was presented: the way of power. Of course my disciples keep getting caught by this one, too. That is why I chose men who did not have power in this world, who were less likely to be trapped by it. But of course all of us can be tempted by it once we have had a taste, the recourse to use power, to make people do what we want, even to force them into the kingdom. It doesn't work. The only way into the kingdom is freedom. It is to come by invitation because one's heart is called, like little children seeing the beauty and the love, and simply walking in. As soon as we use power, we have lost the very thing we had been seeking. God is a self-emptying God. I am walking the way of self-emptying, of surrendering all privilege and power in order to simply invite and give freedom to each one I touch. Come. Come all who are thirsty. Come and eat the richest of fare, drink the living water, without cost and without price. I invite. I can never enforce. The kingdom doesn't work that way. If it did I could call down legions of angels. And even these, my dearest friends, are so slow to learn this. They would like to call down fire from heaven on those who disagree. They would like to hold me back from going to Jerusalem where all the prophets must eventually declare the reality of their truth and their God, that all may see and be drawn, not by force, but by the stirring of their hearts within them. For this I came. To show the compassion and never failing love of my Father, that each may be drawn by that love alone.

Certainly there have been opportunities for me to use power. Men and women have come by their thousands for healing, and to hear the words of the kingdom. Many times I could have taken a position of power. Why, they even tried to make me their king. I could certainly have gone this route. I could have ridden into Jerusalem in triumph and put out the religious leaders, ushered in a new era, set my disciples up as rulers of tens and of hundreds. It is not the way of the kingdom. The way of the kingdom is to give away power, to share power with others, to teach them how to make their own choices, to let them see the Father so they will allow the Spirit to be their guide instead of allowing other men to tell them what to do. The way of the kingdom is the slow way of yeast rising: touching each molecule, rising, one bubble of gas at a time. The way of the kingdom is the winning of each heart, as one seeing a pearl of great price, a treasure hidden, and wanting that treasure more than anything else. The way of the kingdom is the slow and hidden way of a seed sprouting in the ground, brought to life by the living water and the warmth of the sun. The way of the kingdom is by invitation to a feast that takes priority over everything else in one's life. The kingdom is made of each heart, each choice, day by day. That is the only way.

After these temptations were faced and acknowledged, the angels came and ministered to me. I received my Father's comfort and knew his delight in me; I knew his presence. And I knew too the temptations would return again and again, but that God is enough.

I FACE THE SAME DEMONS, FIND THE SAME GOD

Of course, I am challenged by Jesus' words. I have written this only after finding that thirty days of silence indeed made my weaknesses and vulnerabilities rise to the surface and be exposed. As a result, I learned to see that my only recourse is to know myself as a child, in love with the God who invites me to dance. I learned that only in claiming over and over that I am the beloved child of God, that each of us are, can I stay in God's embrace, and see the temptations for what they are. Shortcuts to safety, and significance, and influence are only temporary. I name my own particular ways of seeking the world's comfort, people's approval, and a place of power, and influence. And I surrender them into God's hands. I look to God's eyes alone, for the love that I so deeply need.[3]

---

3. To meditate further on today's relevance of the temptations, see Nouwen's *In the Name of Jesus*. He identifies the temptations as the need to be relevant, the need to be spectacular, and the need to control and be powerful.

14

Coming to the God Who Is

WHAT ARE MY IMAGES?

THIS BOOK is about coming to God, and about using the stories of Jesus so we can imagine ourselves coming to God-in-the-flesh. We take God at his word, that he is enfleshed in Christ so that when we meet the Jesus of the gospels, we are meeting God the Creator, the Omnipresent, the Omniscient—in a way we can handle.

The human mind cannot comprehend the mystery that we call God. The closest we can get is to respond to many different images. The Bible itself is full of different images, different names, in an attempt to represent that which is beyond our grasp.

For each of us, there will be familiar images, safe images, ones that help us come into God's presence. Maybe, indeed, the Jesus we have been journeying within these chapters is a familiar image of God for us. Possibly the Father is a familiar image also, the One Jesus called Abba—implicit in which is intimacy. For some, this image may have difficulties. Especially (although, not necessarily), if their own father had rejected or abused them, or had been distant or absent. For others, the image of a loving father may be the easiest image: a father to whom they could come running, a father whose lap they could climb into. There may also be images we are less likely to have responded to.

> O Jerusalem, Jerusalem, killing the prophets and stoning those who are sent to you! How often would I have gathered your children together as a hen gathers her brood under her wings, and you would not! Behold, your house is forsaken. And I tell you, you will not see me until you say, "Blessed is he who comes in the name of the Lord" (Luke 13:34–35).

What then of the mother, the hen gathering her chicks, the comforting mother[1] of Isaiah 68, or the protective mother bear[2] of Hosea 13? What of the feminine names of God—the feminine Wisdom[3] of Proverbs, El Shaddai[4]—the nurturing God (shad is the word for female breast[5]), and Shekinah the Jewish word for God's abiding presence.[6] What

1. Isa 66:12–13.
2. Hos 13:8.
3. Prov 1, 2.
4. E.g., Gen 17:1, 28:3, 35:11, 43:14, 48:3. Scofield commentary: The etymological signification of Almighty God (El Shaddai) is both interesting and touching. God (El) signifies the "Strong One." The qualifying word *Shaddai* is formed from the Hebrew word "shad," the breast (invariably used in Scripture for a woman's breast). Shaddai, therefore, means primarily "the breasted." God is "Shaddai" because He is the Nourisher, the Strength-giver. http://bibletools.org/index.cfm/fuseaction/Bible.show/sVerseID/399/eVerseID/399/RTD/SCO.
5. Ps 22:9.
6. Shekinah is not a word in the Bible, but it is a Jewish concept taken from the word *shakan*, to abide. Shekinah is a feminine noun denoting God's abiding presence, especially in the Holy of Holies, e.g., Psalm 80:1. It is echoed in the New Testament in Hebrews 9:5. See www.jewishencyclopedia.com and www.ancient-hebrew.org.

of the current recognition that the Holy Spirit is described with many feminine attributes? And what of the God of the creation story who said, "Let us make man in our image," and so "male and female he created them."[7] The God of the Bible includes both genders; images of both genders reflect the mystery of the Creator God.

Many of us may give mental assent to this, and yet when it comes to prayer or imagining God we may revert to the masculine images we have previously learned, or rejected. For many of us, a healing needs to take place to enable us to respond to images of God of both genders. If we have had difficulty with our mothers or other female authority figures, often the feminine images are difficult; even as the male images are difficult for those who have struggled in their relationship with their father. It may be that we simply have never realized that a feminine image of God is orthodox.[8] Or, if we are catholic we may have been taught to pray to Mary as the acceptable female image, instead of finding God as Mother.

Discovering God the Feminine

I have learned much from Julian of Norwich, the thirteenth-century English spiritual mentor[9], who easily moved between genders in her descriptions of the trinity. "The all-Powerful truth of the Trinity is our Father, for he

7. Gen 1:26–27.

8. See also Alexander, *God and Gender*, 116–34.

9. Julian of Norwich is recognized as a Christian mystic and spiritual director. She is most known for her revelations from God, *Showing of Love*, especially the saying, "All shall be well and all manner of things shall be well."

created us and keeps us within him; and the deep Wisdom of the Trinity is our Mother, in whom we are all enclosed; the exalted Goodness of the Trinity is our Lord, and in him we are enclosed, and He in us... all Power, all Wisdom, all Goodness; one God, one Lord."[10] And again, "The mother can give her child suck from her milk, but our precious Mother Jesus can feed us with himself, and he does it most graciously and most tenderly with the Blessed Sacrament, which is the Precious Food of true life."[11]

Julian does not try to explain how God is feminine and masculine—she simply uses the image of Jesus as mother, mixing the genders as though they need not get in the way of our images, and of our coming to God. Other mystics through the centuries have done similarly; they do not let the compartments of the human mind hinder them from coming into God's presence.

Julian seems to be able to respond to God very easily as Father, Mother, Lover. I have not found it so easy. I know that part of it for me has been my own awareness of society's devaluing of women, which somehow I had imbibed and so devalued my own femininity. Somehow it was easier for me to imagine God as my Father, or to come to Jesus as Lover. But for me it felt as though a feminine representation of God was more likely to condemn me. I realized this most specifically when I saw my own criticism of myself as a mother. So I wrote to God, deliberately choosing to accept God as mother, and just wrote what came.

---

10. John Julian, *Complete Julian of Norwich*, 263.
11. John Julian, *Complete Julian of Norwich*, 289.

TALKING TO GOD AS MOTHER

> So then I come Mother God to you, fallen human mother that I am, and say here I am as you know me to be, naked and not covering myself. Coming as a very human mother to you, the only Divine Mother, the only Perfect One, the one who comes in such humility that you kneel at my feet and hold me to your breast, that I may feel your heart beat and know your love outpoured for me—forever outpoured, forever giving, forever in travail, forever in self-giving. This is my God, the One who weeps in self-giving Love.

Meeting God as Mother Changes Me

I have found that the image I have of God influences the way I can relate, just as my images of different people influence the way I relate to them. Coming to God as Mother enabled me to experience myself as feminine in the presence of God's femininity. This is not the same as saying that God is goddess. It is acknowledging the feminine in God as we acknowledge the masculine, the Lover, the protector, the nurturer. And so, by bringing particular struggles I have to God as Mother allows me to experience those difficulties in a different way.

A PRAYER OF RECEIVING

At the end of a day of being in Your presence—your presence Mother God. Finding, instead of shame and condemnation, your nurturing, enfolding love. Love that understands my choices and Love that understands my pain. And somehow holds that, holds me, differently. As though somehow you—the great Feminine—understand my heart's yearning and my heart's pain as a Mother would, as a Woman who has been there would, as a Woman who has loved and known her heart wounded, as One who has given her heart and known the pain of that tearing. And there is no justifying, no condemning, no evaluating—just understanding and holding—holding my heart, knowing I did all I knew, knowing myself not enough—just knowing—and that being enough . . .

15

Lover and Beloved

DARING TO FIND GOD AS LOVER

GOD AS the loving husband seeking his bride is a common metaphor throughout the Bible. It is found even through to the final book where the wedding supper of the Lamb is heralded.[1] It is a metaphor not only for Christ and his church but also for the individual. Song of Solomon is the most obvious example in the Bible of this emphasis on the individual.

The image of God as Lover is one that has been poeticized through the ages. It calls to our inner heart, our inner longings. Some people find the image difficult, especially those who have been hurt by the opposite sex or hurt by a lover, or hurt by sexual abuse. Finding God as the fulfillment of the metaphor can bring healing to the deepest parts of our being.

For some, the strand of sexuality that is part of a lover relationship becomes an issue or a hindrance, as though the sexual part of us is somehow not acceptable in God's presence. It is as if sex was not God's idea in the first place. Genesis makes it clear that sexuality is part of the "good-

1. Rev 19:9.

ness" of creation. It says they were naked and not ashamed; they became one flesh.[2] Parts of the church have gone much astray by judging sexuality as somehow evil or base. The Bible does not teach that celibacy is a more holy state but that it is available only as a choice in order to be more free from the anxieties of the world.[3] Our sexuality is a part of our inner being, and it is part of how we relate, whether those relationships are explicitly sexual or not. Bringing our sexuality into God's presence is an important part of healing.

Coming to God as Beloved allows us to come with the whole of our being into God's presence, and to receive love for the whole of our being. Some men find the metaphor more difficult because their images of God are masculine. Some are able to step past gender compartments as Julian of Norwich was. Some identify themselves as feminine in response to God as masculine. C. S. Lewis suggested we are all female in our relationship with God[4] in the sense that God is the great initiator, and we are always the feminine receiver of his divine initiative. Some thus allow the genders to interchange, as St. John of the Cross was able to do in his Dark Night of the Soul.[5]

> This guided me
> More surely than the light of noon
> To where he waited for me
> Him I knew so well—

2. Gen 2:25.
3. 1 Cor 7:26.
4. Lewis, *Problem of Pain*, 44.
5. Kavanaugh and Rodriguez, *Collected Works of St. John of the Cross*, 358.

> In a place where no one else appeared.
> Oh guiding night!
> O night more lovely than the dawn!
> O night that has united
> The Lover with His beloved,
> Transforming the beloved in her Lover.

For some men this may need some experimentation. For each of us, realizing new possibilities of ways to relate to God takes time and simply being in God's presence.

In reading Song of Solomon, it allows us to take either of the Lover's roles, or even to be the onlookers asking: "What is your beloved more than another beloved, that you thus adjure us?"[6] And then, as though persuaded, "Whither has your beloved turned, that we may seek him with you?"[7]

Experiencing Being the Beloved

The slow reading of Song of Solomon, taking a few verses at a time and experiencing them as though they are indeed my Beloved God speaking his love to me, has been a healing experience for me. Some phrases from chapter one that have caught my attention are listed here:

"O that you would kiss me with the kisses of your mouth! For your love is better than wine . . ."[8]

"Draw me after you and let us make haste. The king has brought me into his chambers."[9]

6. Song 5:9b.
7. Song 6:1b.
8. Song 1:2.
9. Song 1:4.

"I am very dark, but comely . . . Do not gaze at me because I am swarthy, because the sun has scorched me. My mother's sons were angry with me, they made me keeper of the vineyards; but, my own vineyard I have not kept!"[10]

"Behold, you are beautiful, my love; behold you are beautiful."[11]

Another way to put oneself into the scriptural writing—and into an experiential relationship with God—is to allow the words to touch one's heart and then to respond expressively. This may be with words, in poetry or song or reflection. Or it may be with art, painting or drawing. Or it may be with dance or movement.

I find color an important part of expression. Sometimes my painting represents what is expressed realistically. Other times it is just a mix of colors, shapes, and brush strokes, which for me express the words or feelings. Taking the time to work with paints, or movement, or words allows my spirit, soul, and body to drink in the meaning, to let it settle in my heart, and to make my response somehow more tangible and more owned.

I tried to paint Mary Magdalene in the Easter morning garden. It is easy for me to imagine Mary being in love with Jesus. I do not take it further into a sexual relationship. I simply imagine that for a woman healed by him, and in his traveling band, it would be easy for her to love him deeply. I paint her, in his arms, on the first Easter morning. But first, the endless black Saturday. I imagine her then, devastated by his death, waiting with his mother for the Sabbath to pass.

10. Song 1:5a, 6.
11. Song 1:15a.

IDENTIFYING WITH A BROKEN HEART

Now on the first day of the week Mary Magdalene came to the tomb early, while it was still dark, and saw that the stone had been taken away from the tomb. So she ran, and went to Simon Peter and the other disciple, the one whom Jesus loved, and said to them, "They have taken the Lord out of the tomb, and we do not know where they have laid him." Peter then came out with the other disciple, and they went toward the tomb ... Then the other disciple, who reached the tomb first, also went in, and he saw and believed ... But Mary stood weeping outside the tomb, and as she wept she stooped to look into the tomb; and she saw two angels in white, sitting where the body of Jesus had lain, one at the head and one at the feet. They said to her, "Woman, why are you weeping?" She said to them, "Because they have taken away my Lord, and I do not know where they have laid him." Saying this, she turned round and saw Jesus standing, but she did not know that it was Jesus. Jesus said to her, "Woman, why are you weeping? Whom do you seek?" Supposing him to be the gardener, she said to him, "Sir, if you have carried him away, tell me where you have laid him, and I will take him away." Jesus said to her, "Mary." She turned and said to him in Hebrew, "Rabboni!" (which means Teacher). Jesus said to her, "Do not hold me, for I have not yet ascended to the Father; but go to my brethren and say to them, I am ascending to my Father and your Father, to my God and your God" (John 20:1–3, 8, 11–17).

Mary Magdalene:

There is nothing left to live for. We are simply waiting. Waiting through these dreadful, empty, dark Sabbath hours until we can go to his tomb and wrap his body in burial spices. My life is emptied out. There is nothing left to live for. At least we can take care of his broken body. At least wrap it carefully, touch him one more time.

I have slept little. The awful night after the Passover Supper, after they went out to the Mount of Olives. I knew by then, even though I still hoped; but he'd told us so many times by then that he would be taken, and tortured, and crucified. I kept waking through the night, wanting something to change, until someone came and told me where they were holding him; and at least we could go and wait for any little bit of news. And so the whole vile drama played out. I stayed close to Mary. She kept comforting me, telling me these things had to be. Something of her calm at least kept me sane. I don't know how she held such faith. I could see it taking its toll though; she seemed to age as each hour passed. I could hardly think. The other women gathered around too and we cried together, and tried to remember what he had told us. Mary was calmest. She reminded us how she had known since before he was born that his would be a life of wonder and of suffering, and that all was in the hands of the Compassionate Father. I had believed that too, until it all happened, and now the blackness just washes over everything. We followed as they took him out to crucify him, and stood vigil, desperately hoping for some miracle . . . but nothing, unless you count the darkness and the earthquake as he died. Part of me kind of jumped to life. Now they will have to admit he's the Messiah. As if that made any difference now. How can the Messiah die? I kept thinking, how can my Beloved die? He who is the Life-giver. He who has given life to so many. Life itself, dead? I cannot comprehend it. I go off into some daydream as if it will come right, and then I am jerked back into this nightmare reality. Mary strokes my hand. Just trust, she says. But what can I trust for? And the tears start again.

My mind goes around in circles with if-onlys. If only we hadn't come to Jerusalem. If only he hadn't raised Lazarus. If only he hadn't had the crowds shouting as he rode on the colt coming in. If only . . . But he would have come. He kept telling us. I just don't understand. I just want to hold him again. Oh Mary, why keep the Sabbath; why can't we just go? What is the point of keeping the Sabbath now anyway? I just want to go to him. And on and on my thoughts circle around as the day creeps by. One or another of the disciples come by, but no one knows anything; no one can help. We share little details of what we know of his last twenty-four hours. But it's all pointless. It all just runs together in the end: blood, and torture, and tears, and death. And Mary is always calm, even with the tears running down her face. If it weren't for her, I would leave now. I would go and sit in that tomb with him, even though there's that big rock. We saw them roll it over the entrance. And they tell us there are soldiers there guarding it. What are they expecting? Another earthquake? A legion of angels? For Peter and the others to come and steal his body? For what? Anyway, they wouldn't; they're too scared to let their faces be seen. Still, the soldiers would probably let me in. What would they care?

But Mary wants to wait. And so, we wait. Still, I'm going at first light in the morning, maybe before first light. So who's going to see me? That way I'll be there as soon as it is light. I won't have to wait a moment longer.

Someone then gives me something to drink, to calm me down, maybe to make me sleep. It doesn't work. It's as though my body and my mind are never going to work properly again. But then I doze a little, after all. There are some others who have come in. They're going over the same stories . . .

I drowse again, then jerk awake. It's still dark. The candles have burnt very low. People are sleeping. My mind wrenches back to the truth of his death. I'm not going to lie here awake going over it again. I gather up the spices I had prepared, pull my cloak around me, and step around the sleeping bodies. Someone wakes and whispers to me to wait. I don't want to. The tears start again. I'm out the door trying to hurry to the tomb. But it's still very dark and I have to slow down, wondering again how we'll get the stone away—and if the soldiers will be there, and if they will help us if they are. Then, when I finally get there, the stone is gone already and no one is about. Surely none of the men have come already? I look inside. Nothing. They've taken his body away. What shall I do? Who has done this? I run back. It's getting lighter; I can see a bit better. I stumble into the house and there are Peter and John in low conversation. "Have you been already?" I ask. I can see by their lack of understanding they haven't. "They've taken him away! And we don't know where he is." I'm in tears again. They're both out the door and gone before I can say more. I follow them, not hurrying this time. What's the point? I'm nearly there when I meet them coming back. John is saying something about resurrection. Peter is questioning him. They're in earnest conversation. I don't want to join in. I just want to hold him.

I don't know what else to do. I go back to the tomb. Some people are there who I don't recognize. They ask me why I'm weeping. I tell them I don't know where his body is. I ask them if they know anything. Then there's another man behind me. I imagine he's the gardener. He, too, asks me why I'm weeping. And I tell him the same story, and I ask if he knows anything. Then suddenly the most amazing thing happens. He says my name—and all the black emptiness is swept away in light. I'm in his arms clinging as though I will never let go.

I am holding him. His warm living body. My mind has stopped working altogether. I don't understand anything, except that his arms are around me and he is alive. At last he says, "You don't have to keep clinging to me. I haven't gone to the Father yet." I pull back a little and look into his eyes. They are alight with love, even some laughter. "It's all right, Mary. I haven't left yet. And you won't need those spices." He laughs, and it pulls me back into reality. And the sun is well and truly up, and birds are singing. He is alive. I look at him, and the tears are running down my face again even while I'm laughing in joy. But I don't let him go. Finally, he says gently, "Go and tell the others. They don't know yet." The whole world has changed. I still don't want to move. He touches my face. "Mary, it's all right. I will never leave you alone. Go and tell the others." At last I turn, and here I am, telling you: He's alive. He is the Messiah. He is God become human. So we can know his love.

16

Afterword

A Psychological Understanding of the Transformational Process of Ignatian Composition of Place

MARTHA NUSSBAUM, philosopher and scholar, argues that it is our emotions that lead us to ethics, and novels are the genre of the person's ethical formation.[1] As the reader identifies with the character in the novel and follows the story, feeling the joy and the pain, she thus experiences regret over poor decisions, the hope of possible grace, and the satisfaction of good triumphing over evil. Thus we are ethically shaped by the stories of our culture, the imaginary living of the hero's journey, the vicarious grief and delight of each decision played out to its final culmination. It is the stories of our families and our religion, our society, and our nation, which make sense of our world, and model for us how we should then live.

In the same pattern of this initial formation, comes the possibility of transformation. In identifying with different

1. Nussbaum, *Love's Knowledge*, 6.

characters, we experience their anguish and their rejoicing, and we shift our life choices accordingly.

The Ignatian composition of place taps into this transformational process. As we listen with an open heart to several repetitions of a passage, we can be present to it more deeply. As the listener, I am attentive to the story, letting it unfold and waiting for that aspect or person that takes my attention. As I listen again, I identify with a particular character, for example, the rich, young ruler.[2] I try to imagine the real sensory experience—what I smell, see, touch, hear, taste, and feel, the taste of the dust in my mouth as I run and then kneel at the teacher's feet, the smell of the sweaty bodies around me. I see the startled looks as I, a rich man, kneel at the feet of an itinerant preacher. I hear the searching tone in Jesus' voice as he asks, "Why do you call me good?" My senses call me to authentic presence, to really making myself attend to the young man's experience, to make it my own.

To follow a story in vicarious identification, I must touch into the parts of me that are parallel to his story. I go to the part of me that runs like the rich young ruler, to follow God, the part that is willing to publicly declare myself, even to humble myself to kneel in the dust, to know the answer to my question. I tap into my own question, my own longing to live the kingdom most deeply, to live daily in intimate relationship with my king. And I allow myself to be at the feet of Jesus—this man, who more than anyone I have ever heard of, will tell me the truth of the way to life. I let myself feel the hunger to live well, to please God, to make my life count. As I hear Jesus elaborate on the answers our religious culture has given—to keep the commandments,

2. Mark 10:17–22.

not to lie or cheat or steal—I notice my own reactions, that part of me that has tried to do good, that has tried to live a righteous life, not only an externally righteous life, but that part of me that longs to be truly good, inside and out. I notice that even as I declare myself righteous, I still feel the hunger, knowing there is a deeper way of being righteous, of pleasing God, of living in the eternal, kingdom life.

As I see the love in Jesus' eyes and know that all my good intention is seen and acknowledged, I open my heart to hearing what more I need, what more I may be invited into. Even as the rich young ruler, kneeling in the dust of a Palestine street, listens attentively for Jesus' response, I too open myself to what God may say to me. The more I emotionally identify with this young man, the more I feel the power and challenge of Jesus' answer: "One thing you lack." The part of me that hoped for applause feels the blow of his honest appraisal. Yet my awakened longing still waits, wanting to know what hindrances there might be that block my deepest desire. "Go and sell all you have and give it to the poor." As I kneel there with the young man, I know my strongest attachment has been exposed. The light of God shines on the very point of what I hold most tightly, the part of my identity I think I cannot live without.

The naming of riches is a powerful one. Most of us in the West know we would not be willing to give away all we have. It gives us too much power, security, and comfort, which hinders us from giving it away. Even so, most of us, if our hearts are open, know that something else is also named. What is the one thing I lack? What is the one thing I hold most closely: my reputation, applause, recognition, belonging, my job, my position, my family, my talents, my intellectual ability? What would it be like to look into Jesus' eyes of love and have him name this? I am naked yet held in his love in the same moment. And instantly I recognize, too, that there is no manipulation in his love. His naming of my attachment, my addiction, is free of coercion. He loves me whatever my response. I am free to walk sadly away. He will honor me, with letting me go. Thus, there can be no projection, no blame of God being unfair. This is my free choice—to know what holds me, and to know it to be my own responsibility.

My imaginary "being in the story" has led me to a point of transformation. The vicarious experience has become a crucible of honesty and responsibility. I have experienced in the present reality of now, Jesus' love and Jesus' naming of my attachment. The emotion, the going to my own places of longing, of self-righteousness, of hope, has enabled the touch of the Spirit to give me insight, to woo me to a higher way, freeing my will to go towards God or, at least as the rich young ruler did, to know my choices and my resistances as my own.

This process has allowed me to bypass my rationalizations. Even my intellectual understanding, which may be relevant to the story, can sometimes draw me away from the emotional impact the story has while living it from the inside. I have suspended my disbelief and my cognitive resistance, and as I then engage with the story at a deeper level, I allow the Spirit to transform me to the image of Christ; as I see him as he is, I am changed.[3] My listening to a story has become an experiential engagement with the living God in the face of Jesus Christ, the ever-present One.

3. 1 John 3:2.

Bibliography

Alexander, Irene. *Dancing with God: Transformation through Relationship*, London: SPCK, 2007.

———. "God and Gender: The Relational Center." In Myk Habets and Beulah Wood (eds.). *Reconsidering Gender: Evangelical Perspectives*, 116-134. Eugene OR: Pickwick, 2010.

Benner, Juliet. *Contemplative Vision: A Guide to Christian Art and Prayer*. Downers Grove, IL: IVP, 2011.

Johnson, Robert. A. *Owning your own Shadow*. San Francisco: HarperSanFrancisco, 1993.

Julian, John. *The Complete Julian of Norwich*. Orleans, MA: Paraclete, 2009.

Kavanaugh, Kieran and Otilio Rodriguez. (trans). *The Collected Works of St John of the Cross*. Washington: Institute of Carmelite Studies. Revised edition 1991. States: Permission is hereby granted for any non-commercial use, if this copyright notice is included.

Krans, Horatio, S. William Butler Yeats and the Irish Literary Revival. London: Heinemann, 1905.

Ladinsky, Daniel. *Love poems from God*. New York: Penguin, 2002.

Lewis, Clive, S. *The Problem of Pain*. San Francisco: Harper, 2001.

Merton, Thomas. *Thoughts in Solitude*. New York: Farrar Straus Giroux, 1956.

Nouwen, Henri. J. M. *The Return of the Prodigal Son*. London: Continuum, 1996.

Nouwen, Henri. J. M. *In the Name of Jesus: Reflections on Christian Leadership*. New York: Crossroad, 1989.

Nussbaum, Martha. *Love's Knowledge: Essays on Philosophy and Literature*. New York: Oxford, 1990.

Rizzuto, Anna. *The Birth of the Living God: A Psychoanalytic Study*. Chicago: University of Chicago Press, 1981.

www.ingramcontent.com/pod-product-compliance
Lightning Source LLC
Chambersburg PA
CBHW072155160426
43197CB00012B/2393